The ESSENTIALS® of

REGISTERED TRADEMARK

INTERMEDIATE ACCOUNTING I

Eldon R. Bailey, Ph.D.
Chairperson, Department of Accounting
McNeese State University, Louisiana

This book covers the usual course outline
of Intermediate Accounting I. For additional topics, see *"THE ESSENTIALS OF
INTERMEDIATE ACCOUNTING II"*.

 Research and Education Association
61 Ethel Road West
Piscataway, New Jersey 08854

THE ESSENTIALS® OF INTERMEDIATE ACCOUNTING I

Printed in the United States of America

Library of Congress Catalog Card Number 95-71575

International Standard Book Number 0-87891-682-2

ESSENTIALS is a registered trademark of
Research & Education Association, Piscataway, New Jersey 08854

WHAT "THE ESSENTIALS" WILL DO FOR YOU

This book is a review and study guide. It is comprehensive and it is concise.

It helps in preparing for exams, in doing homework, and remains a handy reference source at all times.

It condenses the vast amount of detail characteristic of the subject matter and summarizes the **essentials** of the field.

It will thus save hours of study and preparation time.

The book provides quick access to the important facts, principles, theorems, concepts, and equations in the field.

Materials needed for exams can be reviewed in summary form – eliminating the need to read and re-read many pages of textbook and class notes. The summaries will even tend to bring detail to mind that had been previously read or noted.

This "ESSENTIALS" book has been prepared by an expert in the field, and has been carefully reviewed to assure accuracy and maximum usefulness.

Dr. Max Fogiel
Program Director

CONTENTS

CHAPTER 1

BACKGROUND – ACCOUNTING THEORY AND PRACTICE

1.1 THE CONCEPTUAL FRAMEWORK OF ACCOUNTING

Accounting is an information system for the measurement and communication of financial information about organizations.

Accounting consists of two branches. **Management, or managerial, accounting** provides information for internal users while **financial accounting** is directed towards external users.

The accounting profession consists of two segments: **public accounting** and **internal accounting**. Public accounting refers generally to services provided by certified public accountants (CPAs) including auditing, tax, and management consulting services. Internal accounting involves accountants who perform services within an organization such as general accounting, cost accounting, tax accounting, and internal auditing.

Certified Public Accountants (CPAs) are accountants

who are licensed by a state government to perform public accounting services.

CPAs perform the function of **auditing** financial statements of organizations. This function (often called the **attest** function) provides credibility to financial statements through the expression of an opinion on the fairness of the statements by an independent outside expert in accounting.

The development of accounting theory and practice has been heavily influenced by several organizations:

The **Financial Accounting Standards Board (FASB)** is a private sector organization which has responsibility for the establishment of standards for financial accounting and reporting.

The **American Institute of CPAs (AICPA)** is the major professional organization for CPAs. The AICPA establishes standards for the conduct of audits.

State boards of accountancy license CPAs in the various states and regulate the practice of public accounting in the states.

The **Securities and Exchange Commission (SEC)** is a federal government agency with the responsibility of regulating the interstate sales of securities. The SEC has authority to prescribe accounting and financial reporting standards for those organizations subject to its jurisdiction.

American Accounting Association (AAA). The AAA membership is mainly accounting educators.

National Association of Accountants (NAA). The NAA's activities are mainly in the area of managerial accounting.

Accounting and financial reporting practices are based on guidelines called **generally accepted accounting principles (GAAP).** Generally accepted accounting principles are those principles that enjoy general acceptance as evidenced by substantial authoritative support.

The highest level of authoritative support for an accounting principle is a pronouncement by the Financial Accounting Standards Board or its predecessors, the **Accounting Principles Board (APB)** and the **Committee on Accounting Procedure (CAP).**

Pronouncements of the FASB which establish generally accepted accounting principles are called **Statements of Financial Accounting Standards (SFAS).**

The FASB has conducted a project to delineate the conceptual framework of accounting and has issued **Statements of Financial Accounting Concepts 1-6.**

Concepts Statement Number	Subject
1	Objectives of Financial Reporting by Business Enterprises
2	Qualitative Characteristics of Accounting Information
3	(Replaced by Statement No. 6)
4	Objectives of Financial Reporting by Nonbusiness Organizations
5	Recognition and Measurement in Financial Statements of Business Enterprises
6	Elements of Financial Statements

In addition to the conceptual framework in the concepts statements there are other assumptions, principles, and conventions which are used in accounting. Some of the more important of these are:

Economic entity assumption—A specific entity forms a unit of accountability separate from owners or others. For example, if John Jones is the owner of Jones Furniture Company, the activities of the furniture company would be accounted for separately from Mr. Jones' personal financial activities.

Accounting period assumption—An entity's economic activities may be meaningfully related to periods of time shorter than the entity's life. The effect of this assumption is that financial statements are generally issued by an organization at least annually.

Going-concern assumption—Unless otherwise determined, accounting for an entity is based on the assumption that operations will continue for a reasonable period of time rather than the entity being liquidated in the near future. One effect of this assumption is that financial statements generally present asset values at historical cost rather than at what they could be sold for.

Monetary unit principle—The unit of measure in accounting is monetary units. Measurements are made in nominal units of money. Therefore accounting in the United States, for example, uses the dollar as the measuring unit without making any allowances for changes in the purchasing power of the dollar.

Objectivity principle—To the extent possible, accounting measurements should be based on verifiable evidence. For example, the value of an item is based on a documented sales or purchase transaction rather than on an appraised value.

Historical cost principle—Historical cost is usually the best measure in accounting for goods and services acquired by an entity. Thus, if an item was acquired two years ago for $1,000, it would be accounted for at this amount even though the cost of acquiring such an item at present is $2,000.

Consistency principle—Measurement and disclosure of information about an entity should be on the same basis from one accounting period to the next. Thus, if a particular method was used to value inventory last year, the same method should be used this year.

Conservatism—When alternative supportable solutions to an accounting problem are available, the solution that least favorably affects owners' equity should be favored. For example, in a choice concerning the timing of recognition of a gain which is contingent on some future event, the conservative approach would be to delay recognition of the gain until the future event occurs and confirms the gain.

1.2 THE ACCOUNTING PROCESS

The accounting process is based on the fundamental accounting equation:

> Assets = Liabilities + Owners' equity

These equation elements are defined in **Concepts Statement No. 6** as follows:

Assets are probable future economic benefits obtained or

5

controlled by a particular entity as a result of past transactions or events. Examples of assets are cash, accounts receivable, inventory, land, and buildings.

Liabilities are probable future sacrifices of economic benefits arising from present obligations of a particular entity to transfer assets or provide services to other entities in the future as a result of past transactions or events. Examples of liabilities are accounts payable, notes payable, taxes payable, and bonds payable.

Equity is the residual interest in the assets of an entity that remains after deducting its liabilities. In a business, this residual interest is the **owners' equity**.

The steps in the accounting process (or cycle) are:

1. Identify transactions.

Those transactions, circumstances, and events that affect the fundamental accounting equation are systematically identified. Transactions are usually related to the creation of a document such as a check, invoice, or receipt. Transactions may thus generally be identified by reference to such documents. For example, credit sales transactions for a given period can be identified by reference to the sales invoices for that period.

2. Analyze transactions.

The effects of transactions on the fundamental accounting equation are identified. Details of assets, liabilities, and owners' equity (including revenues and expenses) are kept in records called **accounts**. Accounts are two-sided devices for recording increases and decreases. The left side of an account is named the **debit** side. The right side is the **credit** side.

Changes in account balances are recorded according to the following rules:

Type of Account	Increases	Decreases	Normal Balance
Asset	Debit	Credit	Debit
Liability	Credit	Debit	Credit
Owners' Equity	Credit	Debit	Credit
Revenue	Credit	Debit	Credit
Expense	Debit	Credit	Debit

3. Record transactions in journals.

The effects of a transaction are recorded as debits and credits in a book of original entry called a **journal**. The record of a transaction in a journal is called a **journal entry**. A journal entry lists the accounts affected by a particular transaction with the dollar amount of the debit or credit to each account. The total dollar amount of the debits must equal the total dollar amount of the credits, to maintain the equality of the accounting equation.

A **general journal** can be used for any transaction. **Special journals** may be used for specific kinds of transactions. Common special journals in use are **sales journal, purchases journal, cash receipts journal,** and **cash payments journal.**

An example of a transaction and the resulting general journal entry is:

7

Date	Description	Post. Ref	Dr.	Cr.
Feb. 1	Purchases	501	1,000	
	Accounts Payable	204		1,000
	Purchased merchandise			
	on account from XYZ Inc.			

4. Post to ledger accounts.

A collection of accounts used by an entity is called a **ledger**. The **general ledger** is the collection of accounts which constitute the accounting equation. A list of these accounts is called a **chart of accounts**. Types of accounts are:

Real account—account which remains open, including assets, liabilities, and owners' equity. Example: Cash.

Nominal account—account which is closed at the end of each accounting period, including revenues and expenses. Example: Salaries Expense.

Mixed account—account containing both real and nominal components, which are separated in adjusting entries at the end of the accounting period. Example: Office Supplies Inventory.

Adjunct account—account related to another account, with its balance added to the related account. Example: Premium on Bonds Payable (adjunct to Bonds Payable).

Contra account—account related to another account,

with its balance subtracted from the related account. Example: Allowance for Uncollectible Accounts (contra to Accounts Receivable).

A **Subsidiary ledger** contains accounts which record the details of a general ledger account. For example, the Accounts Receivable account in the general ledger may have a subsidiary ledger containing the accounts of all credit customers. A general ledger account which has a subsidiary ledger is called a **control** account.

The information in journal entries is transferred to the accounts in the ledgers in a process called **posting.**

5. Prepare unadjusted trial balance.

A **trial balance** is a listing of the general ledger accounts with their debit or credit balances. The total of the debit balances must equal the total of the credit balances.

6. Prepare adjusting entries.

The **accrual basis of accounting** recognizes revenue in the period in which it is earned and expenses in the period in which they are incurred. **Adjusting entries (adjustments)** are made at the end of the accounting period to implement the accrual basis.

Typical adjustments required are:

Accrued revenues: Revenues earned but not yet collected. Example: Accrued interest on a note receivable.

Accrued expenses: Expenses incurred but not yet

9

paid. Example: Accrued interest on a note payable.

Deferred (unearned) revenues: Revenues collected in advance, not yet earned. Example: Rent collected in advance.

Deferred (prepaid) expenses: Expenses paid in advance. Example: Insurance premiums paid in advance.

Depreciation: Allocation of part of the cost of a long-lived asset to the current period.

Bad debts: Estimated uncollectible portion of credit sales.

7. Prepare adjusted trial balance.

A second trial balance is prepared listing account balances after adjustment.

8. Prepare financial statements.

The basic financial statements are prepared using the account balances from the adjusted trial balance. The statements are (1) **income statement,** (2) **balance sheet,** and (3) **statement of cash flows.** In addition, a **statement of retained earnings** may be prepared.

9. Prepare closing entries.

Journal entries are prepared to **close**—or reduce the balance to zero—the nominal accounts, and to transfer the net income or loss for the period to equity.

10. Prepare a post-closing trial balance.

A final trial balance is prepared listing the accounts which are not closed, with their balances.

11. Prepare reversing entries.

Some adjusting entries may be reversed at the beginning of the new accounting period. These are entries for accrued expenses, accrued revenues, deferred expenses when originally recorded as an expense, and deferred revenues when originally recorded as a revenue.

Steps 10 and 11 are generally considered optional.

Steps 5, 6, 7, and 8 are usually done informally first through preparation of a **work sheet.**

CHAPTER 2

THE BASIC FINANCIAL STATEMENTS

2.1   THE INCOME STATEMENT

The **income statement** reports the results of operations of the entity for a period of time with a measurement of **net income** or **net loss**. The basic model of the income statement is:

> Revenues − Expenses + Gains − Losses =
> Net Income (or Net Loss)

The elements of this model are defined in **Concepts Statement No. 6** as follows:

Revenues are inflows or other enhancements of assets of an entity or settlements of its liabilities (or a combination of both) from delivering or producing goods, rendering services, or other activities that constitute the entity's ongoing major or central operations. An example is Sales Revenue.

Expenses are outflows or other using up of assets or incurrences of liabilities (or a combination of both) from delivering or producing goods, rendering services, or carrying out other activities that constitute the entity's ongoing major or central operations. An example is Cost of Goods Sold.

Gains are increases in equity (net assets) from peripheral or incidental transactions of an entity and from all other transactions and other events and circumstances affecting the entity except those that result from revenues or investments by owners. An example is Gain on Sale of Equipment.

Losses are decreases in equity (net assets) from peripheral or incidental transactions of an entity and from all other transactions and other events and circumstances affecting the entity except those that result from expenses or distributions to owners. An example is Loss on Sale of Equipment.

The basic components of a **multiple-step** income statement are shown in the following illustration.

X CORPORATION
INCOME STATEMENT
For the Year Ended December 31, 19XX

Sales Revenue		$ xx
Less: Cost of Goods Sold		$ xx
Gross margin on sales		xx
Less: Operating expenses:		
Selling expenses	$ xx	
General & administrative expenses	xx	xx
Income from operations		xx
Other revenues		xx
Less: Other expenses		xx
Income from continuing operations before taxes		xx
Less: Income taxes		xx

13

Income from continuing operations		xx
Discontinued operations:		
Gain on disposal of segment assets (net		
of taxes)	$ xx	
Loss from discontinued segment	(xx)	xx
Extraordinary item (net of taxes)		xx
Cumulative effect of change in accounting		
principle		xx
Net income		$ xx

The **single-step** form of the income statement does not separately list intermediate amounts such as gross margin or income from operations.

X CORPORATION
INCOME STATEMENT
For the Year Ended December 31, 19XX

Revenues:		
Net sales		$ xx
Other revenue		xx
Total revenues		xx
Expenses:		
Cost of goods sold	$ xx	
Selling Expenses	xx	
General & administrative expenses	xx	
Other expenses	xx	
Total expenses		xx
Income from continuing operations before taxes		xx
Less: Income tax expense		xx
Income from continuing operations		xx
Discontinued operations:		
Gain on disposal of segment assets		
(net of taxes)	$ xx	
Loss from discontinued segment	(xx)	xx

Extraordinary item (net of taxes)	xx
Cumulative effect of change in accounting principle	xx
Net income	$ xx

Both income statement models would also shown earnings per share information.

A **Statement of Retained Earnings** is also usually presented for a corporation. The basic statement model is as follows.

X CORPORATION
STATEMENT OF RETAINED EARNINGS
For the Year Ended December 31, 19XX

Retained earnings, January 1, 19XX	$ xx
Less (or add):	
Prior period adjustments (net of tax effect)	xx
Retained earnings, January 1, 19XX, as restated	xx
Add: Net income	xx
Less: Dividends declared	xx
Retained earnings, December 31, 19XX	$ xx

If a corporation also has changes in equity accounts other than retained earnings, a **Statement of Stockholders' Equity** may be prepared to reflect such changes in combination with the changes in retained earnings.

2.2 THE BALANCE SHEET

The **balance sheet** (or **statement of financial position**) reports the financial position of the entity in terms of the basic accounting equation:

Assets = Liabilities + Owners' Equity

Assets, liabilities, and equity are classified on the balance sheet in the following classifications.

Assets: Current assets
             Long-term investments
             Property, plant and equipment
             Intangible assets
             Other assets

Liabilities: Current liabilities
             Long-term liabilities

Equity: Paid-in capital 납입자본
             Capital stock 자본금
               Preferred stock 우선주
               Common stock 보통주
               Paid-in capital in excess of par 주식발행초과금
             Retained earnings

The basic balance sheet model is shown on the following page.

Current assets are cash and other assets which are reasonably expected to be realized in cash or sold or consumed during the normal **operating cycle** of the business or within one year, whichever is longer. The operating cycle (cash to cash cycle) is the time from the investment of cash in inventory until the inventory is sold and cash collected. Example: Accounts Receivable.

Long-term investments are investments and funds that management intends to hold for a longer time than the operating cycle or one year and which are not used in the normal business operations. Example: Investment in C Inc. stock.

Property, plant and equipment includes tangible, long-lived assets that are used in the operation of the business. Example: Buildings.

X CORPORATION
BALANCE SHEET
December 31, 19XX
ASSETS

Current Assets

Cash		$ xx	
Marketable securities		xx	
Accounts receivables	$ xx		
Less: Allowance for doubtful accounts	xx	xx	
Merchandise inventory		xx	
Prepaid expenses		xx	
Total current assets			$ xx

Long-term Investments

Investment in Z Inc. stock		xx	
Investment in land		xx	
Total long-term investments			xx

Property, Plant and Equipment

Land		xx	
Building	xx		
Less: Accumulated depreciation	xx	xx	
Equipment	xx		
Less: Accumulated depreciation	xx	xx	
Total property, plant and equipment			xx

Intangible Assets

Goodwill		xx
Total Assets		$ xx

LIABILITIES AND STOCKHOLDERS' EQUITY

Current Liabilities

Accounts payable		$ xx	
Interest payable		xx	
Unearned rent revenue		xx	
Total current liabilities			$ xx

Long-term Liabilities

Bonds payable		xx	
Less: Unamortized discount 비용성 할인차금		xx	xx
Total Liabilities			xx

Stockholders' Equity

Capital Stock

Common stock ($x par, x shares authorized, x shares issued and outstanding)	xx	
Paid-in capital in excess of par	xx	
Total paid-in capital		xx
Retained earnings		xx
Total Stockholders' Equity		xx
Total Liabilities and Stockholders' Equity		$ xx

Intangible assets are long-lived assets, lacking physical substance, that are used in the operation of the business. Examples are patents and copyrights.

Other assets are assets that do not fit into one of the other asset categories. This category usually should not be needed or used.

Current liabilities are obligations whose liquidation is reasonably expected to require the use of existing resources properly classifiable as current assets or the creation of other current liabilities within the normal operating cycle or one year, whichever is longer. Example: Accounts Payable.

Long-term liabilities are all other liabilities which are payable later than one operating cycle or one year, whichever is longer. Example: Bonds Payable.

Owner's equity reflects the interest of the owners in the assets of the entity. In a corporation, this interest is called **stockholders' equity**. Stockholders' equity is divided into **paid-in capital** and **retained earnings**. Paid-in capital reflects amounts paid by stockholders for shares of stock in the corporation. Retained earnings reflect the undistributed earnings of the corporation. A debit balance in retained earnings is called a **deficit**.

2.3   THE STATEMENT OF CASH FLOWS

A **Statement of Cash Flows** presents information about an entity's cash receipts and cash payments during a period. Cash flows are classified into operating activities, investing activities, and financing activities. The following illustrates the basic model of the statement.

X CORPORATION
STATEMENT OF CASH FLOWS
For the Year Ended December 31, 19XX

Increase (Decrease) in Cash and Cash Equivalents

Cash flows from operating activities:		
Cash received from customers	$ xx	
Cash paid to suppliers and employees	(xx)	
Income taxes paid	(xx)	
Net cash provided by operating activities		$ xx
Cash flows from investing activities:		
Proceeds from sale of facility	xx	
Capital expenditures 자비지출	(xx)	
Net cash used in investing activities		(xx)
Cash flows from financing activities:		
Proceeds from issuance of long-term debt	xx	
Proceeds from issuance of common stock	xx	
Net cash provided by financing activities		xx
Net increase in cash and cash equivalents		xx
Cash and cash equivalents at beginning of year		xx
Cash and cash equivalents at end of year		$ xx

The statement should also include a reconciliation of net income to net cash provided by operating activities.

The above illustration presents the **direct method** of reporting net cash flow. An **indirect method** is also acceptable.

The statement explains the changes in cash and **cash equivalents**. Cash equivalents are short-term, highly liquid investments that are both readily convertible to known amounts of cash and so near their maturity that they present insignificant risk of changes in value because of changes in interest rates.

Investing activities include making and collecting loans and acquiring and disposing of debt or equity instruments and property, plant, and equipment and other productive assets. **Financing activities** include obtaining resources from owners and providing them with a return on, and a return of, their investments; borrowing money and repaying amounts borrowed, or otherwise settling the obligation; and obtaining and paying for other resources obtained from creditors on long-term credit. **Operating activities** include all transactions and other events that are not defined as investing or financing activities. Operating activities generally involve producing and delivering goods and providing services.

CHAPTER 3

CASH

3.1 COMPOSITION OF CASH

Cash, as a financial statement item, is money on hand or on deposit in banks which is available for immediate use. Cash therefore includes coins, currency, checks, travelers' checks, money orders, bank drafts, cashiers' checks, and demand deposits (checking accounts). Savings account balances are also usually considered cash.

Several general ledger accounts are used to account for the items which constitute cash. A separate account is usually used for each checking account. In addition, a **petty cash** account may be used to account for small amounts of coins and currency used to make small payments. A **cash on hand** account may be used to account for undeposited cash receipts.

Cash or cash-related items which do not represent money available for immediate expenditure should not be included in cash. The following are examples.

Cash balances designated by management or restricted by

agreement to a specific use would generally be reported separately from cash. If the use is for a specific aspect of current operations or for payment of a current liability the restricted cash may be classified as a current asset. If the purpose is payment of a long-term liability, the cash balance should be classified as noncurrent.

Certificates of Deposit (CDs) usually should be classified as short-term or long-term investments because of the significant penalties levied for withdrawal of the funds other than at maturity of the CD.

Compensating balances, which a company agrees to maintain in a bank account as support for loans or other credit, should be disclosed either as a separate line-item on the balance sheet or in the notes to the financial statements.

In the accounting for cash, checks written but not mailed or otherwise delivered should not be deducted from cash until they are mailed or delivered.

A **bank overdraft** should usually be classified as a current liability. If the depositor has one or more other accounts in the same bank, the overdraft may be offset against the balance in the other accounts for financial reporting purposes.

Postdated checks and **NSF checks** (deposited checks returned by the bank because the maker does not have sufficient funds on deposit to cover the check) should be considered receivables and not cash.

Postage stamps on hand are not cash but are prepaid expenses.

Deposits in foreign banks that are restricted as to use or

withdrawal and deposits in closed banks should not be classified as cash but as receivables.

3.2   CONTROL OF CASH

Control of cash is important in an organization because cash is essential to the conduct of operations. However, cash is also very vulnerable to misappropriation because in some forms it has no evidence of ownership, is easy to conceal and transport, and is desired by everyone.

Control of cash is achieved through (1) careful planning of cash flows and (2) through a system of **internal control** over cash.

Cash planning involves the **cash budget,** a projection of cash flows and balances. Cash budgeting allows managers to plan for having adequate cash available for operating needs and for investment of idle cash in times of excess cash availability.

Some basic principles of internal control over cash are:

1. The function of custody of cash should be separated from the function of record keeping.

2. Cash disbursements should be made only when authorized and supported by appropriate documentation.

3. Bank accounts should be used. All cash receipts should be deposited intact in bank accounts and all disbursements should be made by check. Book records of cash transactions should be reconciled periodically with bank records.

4. Operate a petty cash fund on an imprest basis with close supervision.

3.3 PETTY CASH

A **petty cash fund** may be established to provide a means for making small expenditures for which the check writing process may be too cumbersome or costly. The fund should operate on an **imprest basis,** meaning that the fund is established for some fixed amount and is replenished only according to amounts expended from the fund.

The procedure for establishing and operating a petty cash fund should be as follows:

1. A person is designated as petty cashier to be responsible for the fund. To establish the fund, a check is written for the fixed amount the fund is to contain. The check is cashed and the money put in the custody of the petty cashier.

2. The petty cashier makes expenditures from the fund as required. For each expenditure, adequate documentation is obtained. The petty cashier should maintain a record of all expenditures.

3. When the fund runs low, the petty cashier requests replenishment of the fund, submitting the documentation for the expenditures made. A check is written in the amount of the total expenditures, with the cash going to the petty cashier to bring the fund back to its established amount.

4. The initial check is recorded with a debit to Petty Cash and a credit to Cash. Replenishment checks are recorded with debits to the expense or other accounts affected by the petty cash expenditures and a credit to Cash.

3.4 RECONCILIATION OF BANK BALANCES WITH BOOK BALANCES

A major advantage of using bank accounts for cash transactions is that a double record of these transactions is obtained. Normally, the bank provides a **monthly bank statement** for each account, showing the transactions recorded in the account that month by the bank. It is very unlikely that the end of the month balance shown on the bank statement will agree with the book balance. A **reconciliation** of the two records should be made to identify any errors or unrecorded items.

The reasons for differences between the bank and book balances of a particular cash account may be classified as follows:

1. Items added to the account on the books but not added on the bank statement. An example is deposits in transit, cash deposited in the bank and recorded on the books but not yet recorded by the bank. Typically, a deposit in transit will be one made late in the day on the last day of the month but not recorded by the bank until the first business day of the next month.

2. Items added on the bank statement but not added to the account on the books. An example is a note receivable collected by the bank for the company. Such a collection may not be recorded on the books until after receipt of the bank statement.

3. Items subtracted from the account on the books but not subtracted on the bank statement. An example is outstanding checks. These are checks written and deducted on the books but which have not yet cleared the bank and been deducted from the bank balance.

4. Items subtracted from the bank balance but not subtracted from the account on the books. An example is a bank service charge. Such charges are typically not known or recorded on the books until after receipt of the bank statement.

The bank statement and book records should be compared to identify the differences between the two records. Then a **bank reconciliation** should be prepared to identify and account for all the differences.

There are two commonly used formats for the bank reconciliation. In one form the bank balance and the book balance are reconciled to an adjusted or correct cash balance. In the other form the bank balance is reconciled to the book balance.

EXAMPLE

Reconciliation to the correct cash balance

Balance per bank, November 30, 19xx	$15,102
Add:	
Deposit in transit, Nov. 30	1,320
	$16,422
Deduct:	
Outstanding checks:	
(List checks here)	2,106
Adjusted balance per bank	$14,316
Balance per books, November 30, 19xx	$11,324
Add:	
Note collected by bank	3,016
	$14,340
Deduct:	
Bank service charges for November	24
Adjusted balance per books	$14,316

EXAMPLE

Reconciliation of bank balance to book balance

Balance per bank, November 30, 19xx		$15,102
Add:		
Deposit in transit, Nov. 30	$ 1,320	
Bank service charges for November	24	1,344
		$16,446
Deduct:		
Outstanding checks (List)	$ 2,106	
Note collection by bank	$ 3,016	5,122
Balance per books		$11,324

After completing the reconciliation, those items which should be recorded in the books must be identified and appropriate adjusting entries made. In the above illustration, the bank service charges and the note collection would require entries in the books.

An expanded form of reconciliation is frequently used by auditors. This form is called a **proof of cash** or **four-column bank reconciliation**. This form consists of reconciliations of four items:

1. Bank statement and book balances at the end of the previous month.

2 Cash receipts on the books and deposits on the bank statement for the current month.

3. Cash payments on the books and deductions on the bank statement for the current month.

4. Bank statement and book balances at the end of the current month.

XYZ COMPANY
PROOF OF CASH
November 19XX

	Oct. 31 Balance	Nov. Receipts	Nov. Payments	Nov. 30 Balance
Per bank statement	$18,357	$80,149	$83,404	$15,102
Deposits in transit:				
Oct. 31	1,588	(1,588)		
Nov. 30		1,320		1,320
Outstanding checks:				
Oct. 31	(1,733)		(1,733)	
Nov. 30			2,106	(2,106)
Adjusted amounts	$18,212	$79,881	$83,777	$14,316
Per books	$15,914	$79,185	$83,775	$11,324
Notes collected by bank:				
October	2,320	(2,320)		
November		3,016		3,016
Bank service charges:				
October	(22)		(22)	
November			24	(24)
Adjusted amounts	$18,212	$79,881	$83,777	$14,316

CHAPTER 4

RECEIVABLES

4.1 ACCOUNTS RECEIVABLE

Receivables in general are claims against others which are expected to result in the collection of cash. **Trade receivables** result from sales of goods and services to customers. Other receivables, such as receivables from officers and employees, are called **nontrade receivables**. In accounting, **accounts receivable** are trade receivables on open account, without a specific written promise to pay. **Notes receivable** are based on notes, which are written promises to pay.

Accounts receivable result from credit sales. The receivables should be recorded at the **net realizable value**, the amount expected to be collectible.

An account receivable resulting from a sale at a list price less a trade discount should be recorded at the net amount after deducting the discount. For example, if an item is sold at a list price of $1,000 less a 30% trade discount, the entry to record the sale would be:

Accounts Receivable	$700	
Sales		$700

A **cash discount** may be offered by some companies to encourage prompt payment by their customers. Two methods of accounting for receivables involving cash discounts are the **net method** and the **gross method**. To illustrate, assume a sale of $1,000 with credit terms of 2/10, n/30 (2% discount if paid within ten days, otherwise pay in thirty days). To record the sale and collection:

NET METHOD		**GROSS METHOD**	
Accounts Receivable 980		Accounts Receivable 1,000	
Sales	980	Sales	1,000

Assume payment within ten days:

Cash	980	Cash	980
Accounts Receivable	980	Sales Discounts	20
		Accounts Receivable	1,000

Assume payment not made within ten days:

Cash	1,000	Cash	1,000
Accounts Receivable	980	Accounts Receivable	1,000
Sales Discounts Not Taken	20		

If allowances are made for returned goods or other factors, Sales Returns and Allowances is debited to reduce net sales and Accounts Receivable is credited. In an industry which experiences a relatively high rate of returns likely to have a material effect on the financial statements, an end-of-period adjustment should be made to recognize estimated returns.

When sales are made with payments to be received in installments over a period of time, that portion of accounts receivable that represents interest or finance charges should be accounted for separately and recognized as revenue as earned with the passage of time.

Some accounts receivable are likely to prove uncollectible. In order to report the receivables at net realizable value, an estimate of the uncollectible amount is necessary. This estimate may be made as a percentage of sales, based on collection experience, or as a percentage of year-end receivables, based on an analysis of individual account balances.

Illustrative entries in the **allowance method** of accounting for uncollectible accounts are as follows:

1. To estimate the uncollectible accounts expense.

Doubtful Accounts Expense	xx	
Allowance for Doubtful Accounts		xx

2. To write off a particular account as uncollectible.

Allowance for Doubtful Accounts	xx	
Accounts Receivable		xx

3. If an account receivable which has been written off is later collected, the write-off entry should be reversed and the collection recorded.

Accounts Receivable	xx	
Allowance for Doubtful Accounts		xx

Cash	xx	
Accounts Receivable		xx

In the **direct write-off method** of accounting for uncollectible accounts, no estimates are made. Instead, accounts are written off in the period when they are determined to be uncollectible. This method is not in conformity with generally accepted accounting principles.

Accounts receivable may be pledged or sold as a means to receive cash earlier than from normal collection. They may be **pledged** as security for a loan or they may be sold to finance companies. The sale of accounts receivable without recourse is commonly referred to as **factoring**.

4.2   NOTES RECEIVABLE

A **promissory note** is a written promise to pay a specified amount of money at a designated time. The one who promises to pay by signing the note is called the **maker**. The one to whom the money is payable is the **payee**. The payee accounts for a note as a **note receivable**, an asset.

Interest-bearing notes state a **principal** or **face** amount and an **interest rate**. The amount payable at maturity of the note is the principal plus the interest for the term of the note.

As an illustration, assume a note with a principle amount of $1,200 and an interest rate of 10%, payable in 90 days. The note is dated November 1, 19x8.

To record the receipt of the note upon sale of merchandise:

Notes Receivable	1,200	
Sales		1,200

To accrue interest, assuming a fiscal year-end on December 31, 19x8:

Interest Receivable
($1,200 x 10% x 2/12)   20
    Interest Revenue   20

To record receipt of payment of the note on January 30, 19x9,
assuming reversing entries were not made:

Cash   1,230
    Interest Receivable   20
    Interest Revenue
    ($1,200 x 10% x 1/12)   10

A **noninterest-bearing note** carries no stated interest rate.
The stated principal, or face amount, of the note includes interest.
The present value of such a note is the face amount discounted
using the current market rate of interest for such notes.

As an illustration, assume a noninterest-bearing note with a
face value of $1,320, payable in one year. The note is dated
November 1, 19x8. The market rate of interest is 10%.

To record receipt of the note upon the sale of merchandise
having a sales price of $1,200:

Notes Receivable   1,320
    Sales   1,200
    Discount on Notes Receivable   120

To accrue interest, assuming a fiscal year end on December
31, 19x8:

Discount on Notes Receivable   20
    Interest Revenue ($120 x 2/12)   20

To record receipt of payment of the note on October 31, 19x9:

33

Cash	1,320	
Discount on Notes Receivable	100	
Notes Receivable		1,320
Interest Revenue ($120 x 10/12)		100

Notes receivable generally are **negotiable instruments**, and thus may be **discounted**, or sold to a third party before maturity. The payee usually must **endorse** the note when it is discounted, which creates a **contingent liability**, meaning the payee must pay the third party at maturity if the maker does not.

The amount received by the payee when a note receivable is discounted, called the **proceeds**, is calculated as follows:

Proceeds = Maturity value of note
(face value plus interest to maturity) – discount

Discount = Maturity value of note x discount rate x time
from date note is discounted to maturity date

As an illustration, assume a note receivable dated September 1, 19x8, with a face value of $1,000, an interest rate of 8%, and a term of 90 days. The note is discounted at a bank on October 1, 19x8. The discount rate is 10%.

Discount = $1,020 x 10% x 60/360 = $17

Proceeds = $1,020 – $17 = $1,003

The entry to record the discounting of the note would be:

Cash	1,003	
Notes Receivable		1,000
Interest Revenue		3

If any discounted notes are unpaid at a balance sheet date, the contingent liability would be disclosed in a footnote.

If the discounted note is **dishonored** (not paid by the maker) at maturity, the payee would have to pay the maturity value to the bank plus any fees charged by the bank. The following entry would be made, assuming a $20 protest fee:

Dishonored Notes Receivable	1,040	
Cash		1,040

A more formal method of accounting for discounting notes receivable incorporates the contingent liability into the accounts, using an account titled **Notes Receivable Discounted**. The entries would be as follows:

Cash	1,003	
Notes Receivable Discounted		1,000
Interest Revenue		3

The note is paid at maturity by the maker.

Notes Receivable Discounted	1,000	
Notes Receivable		1,000

Alternatively, the note is dishonored and paid by the payee.

Dishonored Notes Receivable	1,040	
Cash		1,040

Notes Receivable Discounted	1,000	
Notes Receivable		1,000

CHAPTER 5

INVENTORIES

5.1 NATURE OF INVENTORIES AND INVENTORY COST

Inventories are goods held for sale in the ordinary course of business. For a manufacturing business, inventories also include goods being produced for sale and materials to be used in production.

A merchandising company buys inventory in finished condition and resells it. The inventory account title most commonly used is **Merchandise Inventory**.

A manufacturing company produces goods and sells them. The inventory accounts commonly used in this type of company are:

Raw Materials: Goods that are incorporated into the finished product and can be traced directly to a product. Example: Wood to be used in the manufacture of furniture.

Factory Supplies: Goods that are used in the manufacture of a product but which are not traceable directly to a particular product. Example: Paint used in the manufacture of furniture.

Work in Process: Partially completed goods. Manufacturing costs are accumulated in this account until products are completed.

Finished Goods: Completed products ready for sale. Total costs of manufacture are transferred to this account when goods are completed.

The major inventory accounting issues are the determination of the cost of the goods sold, to be shown on the income statement, and the cost of the inventory on hand, to be shown on the balance sheet.

The acquisition cost of inventory to be resold or used in production consists of all the costs incurred in getting the inventory ready for sale or use. These costs include invoice cost (less trade discounts and cash discounts) and the cost of transportation to the place of sale or use.

The cost of manufactured inventory is determined using a cost accounting system which accumulates and assigns manufacturing costs to inventory. Manufacturing costs consist of:

Direct Materials: Raw materials that can be traced directly to units of production. Example: Wood used in the manufacture of furniture.

Direct Labor: Costs of labor that can be traced directly to units of production. Example: labor costs of employees who cut out the wooden parts for furniture.

Manufacturing Overhead: All other costs required to manufacture the product. Example: Cost of maintaining machinery used in manufacturing furniture.

The measurement of the cost of goods sold and the cost of inventory on hand may be accomplished by one of two inventory accounting systems. In a **periodic inventory system,** an accounting record of the cost of inventory acquired during a period is maintained. At year-end, a physical count of the inventory on hand is made and its cost is determined using an appropriate cost flow assumption. The cost of goods sold is then calculated as follows:

Merchandising Company:

Beginning Merchandise Inventory
+ Net Purchases
= Goods Available for Sale
− Ending Merchandise Inventory
= Cost of Goods sold

Manufacturing Company:

Beginning Finished Goods Inventory
+ Cost of Goods Manufactured*
= Goods Available for Sale
− Ending Finished Goods Inventory
= Cost of Goods Sold

*Cost of Goods Manufactured:

Cost of raw materials used:
    Beginning inventory of raw materials
    + Net raw materials purchases
    − Ending inventory of raw materials
+ Direct labor
+ Manufacturing overhead
= Total manufacturing cost for the year
+ Beginning inventory of work in process
− Ending inventory of work in process
= Cost of goods manufactured

In a **perpetual inventory system,** a continuous accounting record of inventory transactions is maintained. General ledger accounts for Merchandise Inventory or the various manufacturing inventories are maintained with subsidiary ledger accounts for each product or material. The inventory accounts are increased for the costs of inventory acquired and reduced for the costs of inventory used or sold or transferred. The cost of goods sold or used is recognized when the sale or use occurs. The accuracy of the book inventory records should be verified at least once a year through a physical count.

A physical count of inventory should include all inventory items **owned** by the company at the time of the count. **Goods in transit** should be included if title has passed to the purchaser. Passage of title is usually determined by the freight terms. If shipped **FOB Shipping Point,** title passes when the goods are shipped. If **FOB Destination**, title passes on delivery to the buyer. Goods **on consignment** should be included in the inventory of the **consignor.**

5.2 INVENTORY COST FLOW ASSUMPTIONS

Assignment of costs of inventory to cost of goods sold and cost of inventory on hand is complicated by several factors. Identical items of inventory may be acquired at different costs. There is usually a lag between the acquisition of inventory and its sale. It usually is not practical to identify inventory items so that the specific cost of a particular item is known when it is sold or used. Therefore, it is usually necessary to make some assumption about the flow of inventory costs in order to account for the cost of goods sold and inventory on hand.

In a few cases it is possible to use a **specific identification method.** This method is practical only in the case of inventory items which are easily distinguishable from each other. An

39

example is new automobiles which are identified by identification numbers and whose individual cost is known from specific invoice listings.

In most cases, an inventory cost flow assumption must be used. The most commonly used methods are **First-in, First-out (FIFO), Average Cost,** and **Last-in, First-out (LIFO).**

The FIFO method is based on the assumption that the appropriate amount for the cost of goods sold is the cost of the earliest available goods. The ending inventory cost then is based on the cost of the most recently acquired goods.

To illustrate, assume the following inventory information for a particular product.

Date		Number of Units	Unit Cost	Total Cost
Jan.. 1	Inventory on hand	100	$ 8	$ 800
Feb. 18	Purchase	300	9	2,700
July 22	Purchase	400	10	4,000
Nov. 13	Purchase	200	12	2,400
	Goods available for sale	1,000		$9,900

Sales: 300 units on Feb. 25, 400 units on Aug. 23
Inventory on hand, Dec. 31: 300 units

Assuming a periodic inventory system (FIFO):

Cost of goods sold (using the cost of earliest available goods):

100 units @ $8	$ 800
300 Units @ $9	2,700
300 units @ $10	3,000
Total	$6,500

Cost of ending inventory (cost of most recently acquired goods):

200 units @ $12	$2,400
100 units @$10	1,000
Total	$3,400

Summary:

Cost of goods sold	$6,500
Cost of ending inventory	3,400
Goods available for sale	$9,900

Assuming a perpetual inventory system (FIFO) (See table–Page 42).

The assumption in the Average Cost method is that the appropriate amount for the cost of goods sold and the ending inventory should be based on an average of costs.

To illustrate, assume the basic information from the FIFO example.

For the periodic inventory method, a weighted average inventory cost is calculated.

Weighted Average Inventory Cost:

Total cost of goods available for sale / Total units available.

$9,900 / 1,000 = $9.90 per unit

Cost of goods sold	= 700 units @ $9.90 =	$6,930
Ending inventory	= 300 units @ $9.90 =	2,970

41

Date	Purchases	Sales	Balance
Jan. 1			100@$8 $ 800
Feb. 18	300@$9 $2,700		100@$8 800 300@$9 2,700
Feb. 25		100@$8 $ 800 200@$9 1,800	100@$9 900
July 22	400@$10 4,000		100@$9 900 400@$10 4,000
Aug. 23		100@$9 900 300@$10 3,000	100@$10 1,000
Nov. 13	200@$12 2,400		100@$10 1,000 200@$12 2,400 $3,400
Total		$6,500	

Summary:
Cost of goods sold $6,500
Cost of ending inventory 3,400
Goods available for sale $9,900

Summary:

Cost of goods sold	$6,930
Cost of ending inventory	2,970
Goods available for sale	$9,900

For the perpetual inventory method, a moving average cost would be used.

	Purchases	Sales	Balance
Jan. 1			100@$8 $ 800
Feb. 18	300@$9 $2,700		400@$8.75 3,500
Feb. 25		300@$8.75 $2,625	100@$8.75 875
July 22	400@$10 4,000		500@$9.75 4,875
Aug. 23		400@$9.75 3,900	100@$9.75 975
Nov. 13	200@$12 2,400		300@$11.25 3,375
Total		$6,525	

Summary:
Cost of goods sold $6,525
Cost of ending inventory   3,375
Goods available for sale $9,900

The LIFO method is based on the assumption that the appropriate amount for the cost of goods sold is the cost of the most recently acquired goods. The ending inventory cost then is based on the cost of the earliest available goods.

43

To illustrate, assume the basic information from the FIFO example.

Assuming a periodic inventory system (LIFO):

Cost of goods sold (using the cost of the latest available goods):

200 units @ $12	$2,400
400 units @ $10	4,000
100 units @ $9	900
Total (700 units)	$7,300

Cost of ending inventory (cost of earliest available goods):

100 units @ $8	$ 800
200 units @$9	1,800
Total (300 units)	$2,600

Summary:

Cost of goods sold	$7,300
Cost of ending inventory	2,600
Goods available for sale	$9,900

Assuming a perpetual inventory system (LIFO) (See table–Page 45).

Generally accepted accounting principles require that the inventory costing method used should be chosen with the objective of most clearly reflecting periodic income with the matching appropriate costs against revenues. The major argument in favor of FIFO and average cost is that the cost flow assumption approximates the physical flow of goods. The major argument against FIFO and average cost is that, in periods of rising prices,

Date	Purchases	Sales	Balance	
Jan. 1			100@$8	$ 800
Feb. 18	300@$9 $2,700		100@$8	800
			300@$9	2,700
Feb. 25		300@$9 $2,700	100@$8	800
July 22	400@$10 4,000		100@$8	800
			400@$10	4,000
Aug. 23		400@$10 4,000	100 @$8	800
Nov. 13	200@$12 2,400		100@$8	800
			200@$12	2,400 $3,200
		Total $6,700		

Summary:
Cost of goods sold	$6,700
Cost of ending inventory	3,200
Goods available for sale	$9,900

there is poor matching because current (higher) sales prices are matched with older (lower) costs. The poor matching results in reported income which includes inventory holding gains (or "inventory profits") which are not real income since they must be used to replace the inventory at higher costs.

LIFO is supported by some with the argument that this method provides better matching since cost of goods sold is based on more recent purchase costs. Arguments against LIFO include a balance sheet inventory value that does not reflect current values, the possibility of income manipulation by management decisions on buying or not buying inventory, and unreasonable profits in the event of the liquidation of the LIFO beginning inventory layer.

Generally accepted accounting principles require that, regardless of the inventory costing method used, the inventory on the balance sheet must be shown at the **lower of cost or market (LCM).** The LCM rule states that when the utility of goods on hand has declined below its cost, the difference should be recognized as a loss of the current period by writing the inventory down to its market value. **Market value** is defined as the current replacement cost. However, market value may not exceed the net realizable value of the inventory nor be less than the net realizable value less the normal profit margin.

The following is an illustration of the application of the LCM rule.

	Inventory Item #1	Inventory Item #2	Inventory Item #3
Cost	$2.00	$2.00	$2.00
Replacement Cost	2.50	1.50	1.80
Net Realizable Value	3.25	1.40	2.20
Net Realizable Value less Normal Markup	2.25	.90	1.90
Market	2.50	1.40	1.90
Lower of Cost or Market	2.00	1.40	1.90

The LCM rule may be applied to individual items or to the inventory as a whole or to major categories of inventory, whichever application most clearly reflects periodic income.

5.3 OTHER VALUATION AND ESTIMATION PROCEDURES

Application of the LIFO method to individual inventory units will require substantial recordkeeping if the number of different inventory items is large. To reduce the recordkeeping effort and for other reasons, the LIFO method may be applied to **inventory pools.** Similar inventory items are grouped together in a pool to which an inventory accounting method is applied.

An inventory method used with inventory pools is **dollar-value LIFO.** The inventory at the end of the period is first valued at current cost. If this cost is different from the beginning inventory value, the change may be the result of changes in costs or quantity or both. The dollar-value LIFO method isolates the change in cost so that the real increase or decrease in inventory quantity may be measured. If the quantity has increased, a new **inventory layer,** valued at current costs, is added to the beginning inventory to determine the value of the ending inventory. If the quantity has decreased, previous LIFO layers are removed from inventory, starting with the most recently added layer.

The following is an illustration of the dollar-value LIFO method.

Step 1. Value the ending inventory at current prices.

Assume ending inventories at current prices as follows:

19x1	$20,088
19x2	21,712

47

Assume the beginning inventory 19x1 is $18,000.

Step 2. Convert the ending inventory to base year prices, using a conversion index.

The formula for the conversion index is:

> Conversion index =
> Base year price index / Current price index

The price indexes used may be relevant published indexes or indexes determined by the **double-extension technique.**

If the double-extension technique is used, a sample of ending inventory at current prices is compared to that sample at base year prices.

$$\text{Current price index} = \frac{\text{Sample of ending inventory at current prices}}{\text{Sample of ending inventory at base year prices}}$$

EXAMPLE

A representative sample of the inventory pool items:

	Current Prices	Base Year Prices	Current Price Index
19 x 1	$6,480	$6,000	$6,000/$6,480 = 108
19 x 2	7,080	6,000	$6,000/$7,080 = 118

Ending inventories at base year prices:

19x1: $20,088 x 100/108 = $18,600
19x2: $21,712 x 100/118 = $18,400

Step 3. Determine the change in inventory quantity for the year at base year prices by comparing the ending inventory at base year prices with the beginning inventory at base year prices.

19x1: Ending inventory at base year prices:

$20,088 x 100/108 = $18,600

Change in inventory quantity at base year prices:

$18,600 – $18,000 = +$600

19x2: Ending inventory at base year prices:

$21,712 x 100/118 = $18,400

Change in inventory quantity at base year prices:

$18,400 – $18,600 = – $200

Step 4. Add an inventory layer if there is an increase in quantity at base year prices or remove layer(s) or part of a layer if there is a decrease. A layer is added at current prices. Removal of layers starts with the most recently added layer.

19x1: Ending inventory:

$18,000 x 100/100	$18,000
600 x 108/100	648
Total	$18,648

19x2: Ending inventory:

$18,000 x 100/100	$18,000
400 x 108/100	432
Total	$18,432

An alternative method for determining the current price index is the link-chain technique. A sample of the ending inventory at current year prices is compared to that sample at last year's current prices. That ratio is multiplied by the price index at the end of the previous year to determine the current year index.

The **retail inventory method** is a method for estimating inventory and cost of goods sold amounts using information on the relationship between inventory costs and selling prices.

The following terminology is used in the retail inventory method.

Markup—the amount originally added to cost to determine selling price.

Additional markup—an amount added to the original selling price.

Markup cancellation—a cancellation of all or part of an additional markup.

Net markup—additional markups less markup cancellations.

Markdown—reduction in original selling price.

Markdown cancellation—cancellation of all or part of a markdown.

Net markdown—markdowns less markdown cancellations.

The most commonly used version of the retail inventory method, sometimes called the conventional retail method, produces an ending inventory amount which approximates the **lower of average cost or market.** This method is illustrated below.

	At cost		At retail
Beginning inventory	$1,000		$1,500
Net purchases	600		900
Additional markups		$200	
Less: Markup cancellations		100	
Net markups			100
Goods available for sale	$1,600		$2,500

Cost/retail ratio:

$1,600/$2,500 = 64%

Deduct:			
Sales			(1,800)
Markdowns		$300	
Less: Markdown cancellations		100	
Net markdowns			(200)

Ending inventory:
At retail			$ 500
At lower of cost or market:			
$500 x 64%		$ 320	

The conventional retail method illustrated above approximates average lower of cost or market by including the beginning inventory and markups in the calculation of the cost/retail ratio but excluding markdowns. Other variations of the retail method are:

Average cost—includes beginning inventory and both markups and markdowns in cost/retail ratio.

51

FIFO cost—excludes beginning inventory but includes both markups and markdowns in calculation of cost/retail ratio.

FIFO lower of cost or market—excludes beginning inventory, includes markups but excludes markdowns in calculation of cost/retail ratio.

The retail inventory method may also be used to determine inventory at LIFO. If inventory increases, a new layer is added at the cost/retail ratio for purchases for the period. If inventory decreases, the inventory reduction is calculated at the cost/retail ratio of the beginning inventory.

The following is a simple illustration of the LIFO retail method. The $40 increase in inventory at retail is added to the beginning inventory at the cost of this period's purchases.

	Cost	Retail	
Beginning inventory	$ 96	$160	Ratio = 60%
Net purchases	260	400	Ratio = 65%
		$560	
Sales		360	
Ending inventory at retail		$200	
Ending inventory at cost:			
Beginning layer	$ 96		
New layer: $40 x 65%	26		
Total	$122		

If the ending inventory at retail were $140, a $20 decrease, the ending inventory would be $140 x 60% = $84, using the cost/retail ratio of the beginning inventory.

The **retail dollar-value LIFO method** is a combination of the retail method and dollar-value LIFO. The steps in this method are as follows:

1. Determine the ending inventory at current retail prices and convert to base year retail prices using the current year conversion index.

2. Subtract ending inventory at base year retail prices from beginning inventory at base year retail prices to determine the change in inventory quantity in base year retail prices.

3. If the inventory has increased, add a new layer. Convert the change in base year retail prices to current year retail prices by multiplying by the current year price index. Convert the increase at retail to cost by multiplying by the current year cost/retail ratio for current year purchases. If inventory has decreased, the ending inventory comes from the beginning of the year inventory layers on a LIFO basis.

ILLUSTRATION

Assumptions:

Beginning inventory	Cost	$ 7,200
	Retail	12,000
	Cost/Retail ratio = 60%	
	Price index = 100	

Ending inventory at retail $15,400
Cost/Retail ratio for current year purchases = 75%
Current year price index = 110

Step 1. $15,400 x 100/110 = $14,000 (EI at base year retail)

Step 2. $14,000 – $12,000 = $ 2,000 (Increase at base year retail)

53

Step 3. $2,000 x 110/100   = $ 2,200 (Increase at
                                                current retail)

          $2,200 x 75%   = $1,650 (New layer at cost)

Ending inventory at cost:
    Beginning inventory layer $7,200
    New layer   1,650
    Total $8,850

If the ending inventory at retail were $11,000:

Step 1. $11,000 x 100/110   = $10,000 (EI at base
                                                year retail)

Step 2. $10,000 – $12,000   =   –$2,000 (Decrease at base
                                                year retail)

Step 3.   Deduct beginning inventory layer:
          $12,000 – $2,000   = $10,000 (EI at base
                                                year retail)
          $10,000 x 60%   = $ 6,000 (EI at cost)

The **gross profit method** is a technique for estimating the
cost of ending inventory. The method is not acceptable under
generally accepted accounting principles for annual financial
statements. It may be used, however, for estimating inventories
for interim financial statements and for special purposes such as
testing the reasonableness of inventory figures and estimating the
cost of inventory destroyed by fire or other casualty.

An illustration of the computation under the gross profit
method is as follows:

Beginning inventory		$10,000
Purchases		40,000
Goods available for sale		$50,000
Cost of goods sold:		
Sales	$36,000	
Less: Gross profit of 30%	10,800	25,200
Estimated ending inventory		$24,800

This illustration assumes the gross profit percentage or markup is stated as a percentage of the selling price. If the markup is stated as a percentage of cost, the cost of goods sold is calculated as sales divided by 1 + markup percentage.

For example, if sales are $36,000 and the markup is 60% of selling price, the cost of goods sold would be $36,000 / 1.60 = $22,500.

Errors may occur in valuation of inventories for reasons such as incorrect count, incorrect pricing, or failure to record purchases in the correct period. The correction of such errors requires careful analysis of their effects. For example, an overstatement of the ending inventory in the current year causes an understatement of cost of goods sold and therefore an overstatement of net income. Also, on the balance sheet, assets and retained earnings are overstated. Since the ending inventory of this year becomes the beginning inventory of the next year, the financial statements of the next year will also be affected.

In the acquisition of inventory, companies sometimes enter into unconditional purchase commitments at a fixed price. If a company has such a commitment at a price which exceeds the current market price, the company must recognize a loss, as though it already owned the inventory.

55

EXAMPLE

A noncancellable commitment to purchase inventory at a fixed price of $300,000.

Market price of such goods at end of current year: $250,000

Adjusting entry:

Loans on Purchase Commitments	50,000	
Accrued Liability on Purchase		
Commitments		50,000

Entry when goods are actually purchased:

Purchases (or Inventory)	250,000	
Accrued Liability on Purchase		
Commitments		50,000
Accounts Payable		300,000

Inventories should be reported on the balance sheet as current assets. Footnote disclosure is required for the cost flow method used and the basis for pricing the inventory.

CHAPTER 6

INVESTMENTS

A company may invest in income-producing securities, such as stocks and bonds, issued by another company. The major accounting issues associated with such investments are classification on the balance sheet and measurement of asset value and income.

6.1 INVESTMENTS IN EQUITY SECURITIES

Investments in equity securities may be classified as current assets or long-term investments, depending on the nature of the investment.

The chart on the next page summarizes the classification and accounting methods for investments in equity securities.

MARKETABLE EQUITY SECURITIES

Equity securities are considered **marketable** if the security is traded on a national securities exchange or in the over-the-counter market. The accounting for **marketable equity secu-**

Purpose of Investment	Marketable or not Marketable?	Classification	Accounting Method
1. To obtain significant influence over investee	Either	Non-current	Equity
2. Purposes other than obtaining significant influence	Not marketable	Non-current	Cost
3. Temporary investment to be held less than one year (or operating cycle, if longer)	Marketable	Current	Lower of cost or market
4. Investment to be held more than one year	Marketable	Non-current	Lower of cost or market

rities (not held for the purpose of exercising significant influence) is governed by **SFAS 12**. The basic requirement is that each portfolio (current or non-current) be accounted for at the **lower of aggregate cost or market.**

Application of the lower of cost or market method to a company's portfolio of marketable equity securities may be illustrated as follows.

Assume a portfolio of **current** marketable equity securities, all acquired in 19x1:

Stock	No. Shares	Cost	Market Value 12/31/x1
A Inc.	100	$ 1,500	$1,300
B Inc.	500	10,000	10,125
C Inc.	300	2,400	2,100
Totals		$13,900	$13,525

Since the total market value is less than the total cost, an **unrealized loss** must be recognized. The adjusting entry would be:

Unrealized loss on current marketable equity securities	375	
Allowance to reduce current marketable equity securities to market		375

Assume that during 19x2 there are no sales or acquisitions in the portfolio and that the total market value at 12/31/x2 is $13,000. The adjustment would be:

Unrealized loss on current marketable
    equity securities   525
       Allowance to reduce current
         marketable equity securities
         to market   525

Assume that at 12/31/x3, the total market value of the portfolio is $13,600. The allowance account must be reduced to recognize the increase in the market value of the portfolio and an **unrealized gain** or **loss recovery** is recognized.

Allowance to reduce current marketable
    equity securities to market   600
       Unrealized gain on marketable
         equity securities   600

The unrealized loss or gain on this **current** portfolio would be reported on the income statement. The allowance account would be deducted from cost and reported on the balance sheet on December 31, 19x3, as follows:

Current Assets:
Investment in marketable equity
    securities $13,900
Less: Allowance to reduce to market   300 $13,600

Realized gains or losses are recognized when securities in the portfolio are **sold**. Realized losses are also recognized when an individual security is transferred between the current and non-current portfolios when the security's market value at the time of transfer is below cost, or when a security is written down below cost because of a **permanent decline** in its market value.

Assume that during 19x4, 200 shares of the B Inc. stock are sold for $4,200.

Cash	4,200	
Marketable equity securities		4,000
Gain on sale of investments		200

The portfolio at the end of 19x4 would be as follows, with the assumed market value at December 31, 19x4.

Stock	No. Shares	Cost	Market Value 12/31/x4
A Inc.	100	$1,500	$ 1,600
B Inc.	300	6,000	6,300
C Inc.	300	2,400	2,700
Totals		$9,900	$10,600

Since the aggregate market value at 12/31/x4 is above cost, the allowance balance of $300 should be eliminated and the loss recovery recognized.

Allowance to reduce current marketable equity securities to market	300	
Unrealized gain on marketable equity securities		300

Application of the lower of cost or market rule to a non-current portfolio of marketable equity securities (not held for the purpose of exercising significant influence) would be the same as the above illustration, **except** that an unrealized loss would **not** be shown on the income statement, but would be reported as a **negative stockholders' equity amount.** Recoveries of unrealized losses previously recognized would reduce the balance of the negative stockholders' equity account.

THE EQUITY METHOD

Investments in equity securities may be made for the purpose

61

of exercising **significant influence** over the investee company. This ability is generally acquired through ownership of enough voting stock. The Accounting Principles Board stated that an investment of 20% or more of the voting stock should lead to a presumption, in the absence of evidence to the contrary, of the ability to exercise significant influence. **APB Opinion 18** prescribes the use of the equity method in accounting for such investments.

Under the equity method, the investment is recorded at cost. However, because of the special relationship between the investor and investee, the investment account should be periodically adjusted for changes in the investee's equity underlying the investment.

The basic steps in the equity method are illustrated below.

Assume purchase of 25% of the voting stock of an investee for $100,000.

| Investment in X Company | 100,000 | |
| Cash | | 100,000 |

The investee reports income of $80,000 for the current year.

| Investment in X Company | 20,000(25% x $80,000) | |
| Equity in investee income | | 20,000 |

The investee declares dividends of $20,000.

| Dividends receivable | 5,000(25% x $20,000) | |
| Investment in X Company | | 5,000 |

Adjustment of the amount of investee income recognized by

the investor may be necessary if the cost of the investment was more or less than the investee's book value at the date of acquisition of the investment.

For example, assume that for the illustration above the investor paid $100,000 for the 25% interest when the book value of the investee's net assets was $320,000, and 25% is therefore $80,000. The $20,000 excess ($100,000 − $80,000) is determined to be attributable to the current value of investee's plant and equipment assets being greater than their book value. The undervalued assets have a remaining useful life of ten years. The $20,000 then would be amortized over the ten years and the investor's equity in investee's income reduced by $2,000 per year. The adjusting entry would be:

Equity in investee income	2,000	
Investment in X Company		2,000

CONSOLIDATED FINANCIAL STATEMENTS

An investment may be made for the purpose of acquiring control of another company. Control is accomplished through ownership of more than 50% of the voting stock. In these circumstances, the investor is a **parent company** and the investee is called a **subsidiary company.** Although legally the parent and subsidiary are separate companies, in substance they are one economic entity. Generally accepted accounting principles usually require that the substance be recognized with **consolidated financial statements.** Such statements report the consolidated financial position, results of operations, and cash flows for the companies in one set of statements. These statements result from combining the separate statements of the companies and eliminating intercompany transactions to recognize that, in substance, the companies are one economic entity.

63

6.2 INVESTMENTS IN DEBT SECURITIES

Investments in debt securities are classified as **current assets** if the investment is **temporary** and the securities are **marketable**. Investments in debt securities whose maturity date is current may also be classified as current assets. Investments in debt securities should be classified as **noncurrent assets** or **long-term investments** if (1) management intent is to hold the investment long-term, or (2) the debt securities are not marketable and the maturity date is not current.

Current investments in debt securities should be recorded at cost. No premium or discount is recognized. Interest income is recognized on the basis of the stated rate of interest, without adjustment for amortization of premium or discount. A realized gain or loss is recognized when the securities are sold. No write-down of the investment to market value is made unless the decline in value is determined not to be due to a temporary condition.

Illustration of accounting for current investment in debt securities:

Bonds with a face value of $100,000 are purchased for $103,000 on an interest date. The bonds pay interest semiannually at the rate of 12%.

Investment in bonds	103,000	
Cash		103,000

The company's accounting period ends on December 31, four months after purchase of the bonds.

Accrued interest receivable		
($100,000 x 12% x 4/12)	4,000	
Interest revenue		4,000

Six months' interest is received on the next interest date. Assume that reversing entries were not made.

Cash	6,000	
Accrued interest receivable		4,000
Interest revenue		2,000

Two months later the bonds are sold for $102,500 plus accrued interest.

Cash	104,500	
Loss on sale of investments	500	
Investment in bonds		103,000
Interest revenue		2,000

Accounting for long-term investments in debt securities requires the recognition of premium or discount. Interest income is measured on the basis of the effective rate of interest. This measurement is accomplished by amortizing the premium or discount.

Assume a long-term investment in bonds with a face value of $100,000, and a stated interest rate of 12% and a maturity date five years after acquisition. Interest is payable semiannually and the bonds are purchased on an interest date. The bonds are purchased to yield an effective interest rate of 10%. The theoretical purchase price then would be the present value of the future cash flows on the investment discounted at 10%.

7.

Purchase price:

PV of interest (10 payments of $6,000) discounted at 5% (semiannual rate)	$ 46,330
PV of maturity value $100,000 discounted at 5%	61,391
Total	107,721

65

Entry for purchase of investment:

Investment in bonds	107,721	
Cash		107,721

The premium (or discount) on long-term investments in bonds should be amortized using the **effective interest method**. An amortization table for the illustration appears on the next page.

The journal entry to record the interest received at the first interest date would be:

Cash	6,000	
Interest revenue		5,386
Investment in bonds		614

If the bonds had been purchased at a discount, the effective rate of interest would be greater than the cash rate. The carrying value of the investment would be less than the maturity or face value and the amortization of the discount would reflect interest revenue greater than the cash interest received.

Cash	XX	
Investment in bonds	XX	
Interest revenue		XX

Assume further that after collection of the fifth interest payment on the bonds in the illustration, the bonds are sold for $103,000. The entry would be:

Cash	103,000	
Loss on sale of investments	1,328	
Investment in bonds		104,328

(1) Interest Payment Number	(2) Cash Interest Received (6% x $100,000)	(3) Interest revenue (5% x carrying value)	(4) Premium Amortization (2 − 3)	(5) Carrying Value (Prev. CV − 4)
Acquisition				$107,721
1	$6,000	$5,386	$614	107,107
2	6,000	5,355	645	106,462
3	6,000	5,323	677	105,785
4	6,000	5,289	711	105,074
5	6,000	5,254	746	104,328
6	6,000	5,216	784	103,544
7	6,000	5,177	823	102,721
8	6,000	5,136	864	101,857
9	6,000	5,093	907	100,950
10	6,000	5,050*	950*	100,000

* To amortize balance of premium. Not exact because of rounding.

6.3 OTHER INVESTMENT ACCOUNTING PROBLEMS

투자회계문제

Stock warrants give the holder the right to purchase shares of stock at a stated price. An investor may acquire stock warrants in connection with another security such as a bond or preferred stock. The total price paid must be allocated between the warrants and the other security, normally on the basis of the relative market values of each security. 상대적 시장가치 안분

For example, assume the purchase of $100,000 face value bonds for $106,000. With each $1,000 bond the investor also received 10 detachable stock warrants. Each warrant may be used to purchase one share of common stock. The market value of the bonds without the warrants is $1,040 each. The market value of the warrants is $5 each. The purchase price of $106,000 would be allocated as follows:

$$\frac{\text{Market value of warrants}}{\text{Market value of warrants and bonds}} \times \$106{,}000 = \text{Cost of warrants}$$

$$\frac{\text{Market value of bonds}}{\text{Market value of warrants and bonds}} \times \$106{,}000 = \text{Cost of bonds}$$

$$\frac{10 \times 100 \times \$5}{(10 \times 100 \times \$5) + (100 \times \$1{,}040)} = \frac{\$5{,}000}{\$109{,}000} \times \$106{,}000$$

$$= \$4{,}862.38 = \text{Cost of warrants}$$

$$\frac{10 \times \$1{,}040}{(10 \times 100 \times \$5) + (100 \times \$1{,}040)} = \frac{\$104{,}000}{\$109{,}000} \times \$106{,}000$$

$$= \$101{,}137.62 = \text{Cost of bonds}$$

The entry to record the purchase would be:

Investment in bonds	101,138	
Investment in stock warrants	4,862	
Cash		106,000

Assume that later one-half of the warrants are exercised to purchase 500 shares of stock at $20 per share:

Investment in stock	12,431	
Cash		10,000
Investment in stock warrants		2,431

Assume that 200 of the warrants are sold at $6 each:

Cash	1,200	
Investment in stock warrants		
(20% x 4,862)		972
Gain on sale of investments		228

Assume that the remaining 300 warrants expire.

Loss on Expiration of Stock Warrants	1,459	
Investment in stock warrants		1,459

Stock rights are issued by a corporation to current shareholders in connection with a new issue of stock. The rights allow the stockholders to retain their proportionate interest by exercising the rights and buying additional stock. Alternatively, a stockholder may decide to sell the rights rather than exercise them. When rights are received by an investor, the original cost of related stock should be allocated between the stock and the rights on the basis of the relative market value of each.

A corporation may purchase life insurance on its executives with the company as beneficiary. The insurance policies may accumulate **cash surrender values.** The amount charged as Insurance Expense each year should be the amount of the annual premium less any increase in cash surrender value that occurs during the year. The cash surrender value should be reflected on the balance sheet as a long-term investment.

CHAPTER 7

PROPERTY, PLANT AND EQUIPMENT

Relatively long-lived assets which are used in the operations of an organization are usually referred to in accounting as **property, plant, and equipment.** Expenditures for items such as land, buildings, equipment, and natural resource deposits are **capitalized,** or recorded as assets, because the assets acquired are expected to provide benefits beyond the current accounting period. The benefit is received through the use of the assets in the normal activities of the organization. The cost of such assets is **allocated** to the periods in which the benefit from use of the assets is received through a process called **depreciation, amortization** or **depletion,** depending on the nature of the asset.

7.1 ACQUISITION OF PROPERTY, PLANT, AND EQUIPMENT

Property, plant, and equipment assets are recorded at acquisition at **historical cost.** The cost of such assets is the total of all costs incurred to get the asset ready for its intended use in the operation of the entity. For example, the cost of **land** would include items such as the purchase price, commissions and legal fees associated with the purchase, cost of surveys, and the cost of removing unwanted structures. The cost of **buildings** would include items such as the purchase price and the cost of remodeling to get the building ready for its intended use. The cost of **machinery and equipment** would include items such as the purchase price, costs associated with getting the asset to the place of intended use (freight charges, for example), costs of installation, and costs of trial runs necessary to get the asset into regular operation.

When a **cash discount** is offered for early payment of the purchase price for an asset, theoretically the cost of the asset is the purchase price less the discount, whether the discount is taken or not. Any discount not taken should be recognized as an expense (discounts lost).

Determination of the cost of an operating asset is often complicated by specific problems associated with acquisition of the asset, as discussed below.

ASSETS ACQUIRED WITH LONG-TERM FINANCING

Assets such as buildings and machinery are often acquired with long-term financing such as bonds or long-term mortgage loans from banks or other financial institutions. In such cases, a distinction must be made between the cost of the asset and interest charges for the financing arrangement. The accounting in this situation depends on the circumstances, as illustrated below.

1. The cash purchase price for the asset and the interest rate on the long-term obligation are known.

Assume a purchase of equipment which has a cash purchase price of $500,000. Payment for the equipment will be made in 10 annual payments of $88,492. The installment note carries an interest rate of 12% annually.

The entry to record the purchase of the equipment:

| Equipment | 500,000 | |
| Installment Notes Payable | | 500,000 |

The entry for the first installment payment:

Interest Expense	60,000	
(Interest for one year at 12% per year on unpaid balance of $500,000)		
Installment Notes Payable	28,492	
($88,492–$60,000)		
Cash		88,492

Alternatively, a discount account might be used.

Equipment	500,000	
Discount on Installment Notes Payable	384,920	
Installment Notes Payable		884,920
(10 x $88,492)		

Interest Expense	60,000	
Installment Notes Payable	88,492	
Cash		88,492
Discount on Installment Notes Payable		60,000

2. Neither the cash price (fair market value) of the equipment nor the market value of the installment note are known.

Assume a purchase of equipment. Payment is to be 10

annual installments of $88,492. No interest is stated on the note. The current market rate of interest on such installment purchases of equipment is 12%.

The present value of the 10 installments of $88,492, discounted at 12% interest, is $500,000. This amount should be recorded as the cost of the equipment and the interest expense recognized as in the previous illustration.

Other combinations of circumstances are possible. The basic accounting principle that must be followed is that any interest in the payment for the asset must be accounted for separately from the acquisition cost of the asset. It may be necessary to **impute** interest, as in the second example above.

SELF-CONSTRUCTED ASSETS AND CAPITALIZATION OF INTEREST

Special rules apply to accounting for **self-constructed assets**, particularly with respect to **capitalization of interest** (including interest as part of the cost of the asset).

The cost of materials and direct labor used in constructing an asset clearly should be part of the cost of the asset. There are differences of opinion on the amount of overhead, if any, that should be included. One position is that self-constructed assets should be charged with overhead on the same basis as other company manufacturing or construction activities are charged. A second position is that self-constructed assets should only be charged with **incremental** overhead, the increase in overhead attributable to the construction of the asset. A third position is that **no** overhead should be charged. Official pronouncements do not establish a rule on the overhead issue. Professional judgment would be exercised by an accountant in determining the appropriate cost, depending on circumstances.

SFAS 34 requires that interest incurred during the period an asset is being constructed or prepared for its intended use be capitalized as part of the cost of the asset. To qualify for interest capitalization, an asset must be constructed over an extended period during which significant expenditures take place and interest is incurred. The amount of interest to be capitalized is the interest actually incurred that could have been avoided had the expenditures on construction of the asset not been made. The interest rate to use first is the rate on borrowings specifically for the asset. Otherwise, a weighted average interest rate is used. Interest is charged on the **average accumulated expenditures**. Interest capitalized cannot exceed interest actually incurred.

To illustrate, assume the following:

A company is constructing a building for its own use.

Accumulated expenditures, Jan. 1, 19x1,
  including previously capitalized interest $2,000,000
Accumulated expenditures, Dec. 31, 19x1   3,000,000

During 19x1, $500,000 was borrowed at 12% specifically for this construction project.

The company has other debt outstanding with the average interest rate being 11%.

Total interest incurred on all debt in 19x1 $435,000
To calculate amount of interest to capitalize:

Determine average accumulated expenditures:

Accumulated expenditures: Jan. 1, 19x1 $2,000,000
                           Dec. 31, 19x1   3,000,000
   Total $5,000,000

Average = $5,000,000/2 = $2,500,000

To calculate interest to be capitalized:

Specific borrowing	$500,000 x 12%	$ 60,000
Other debt	$2,000,000 x 11%	220,000
Total		$280,000

(which does not exceed total interest incurred)

Entry (assuming adjusting entry at end of period):

Building	280,000	
Interest expense		280,000

BASKET PURCHASE

A **basket purchase** is the purchase of several assets for one lump-sum price. The total price may be less than the total of the market values of the individual assets. In this case, the purchase price must be apportioned to the individual assets, usually on the basis of their relative market values.

For example, assume a company purchases the land, buildings, equipment, and inventory of another company which is going out of business. The lump-sum purchase price is $1,215,000. Apportionment of this price according to relative market value would be:

Asset	Current Market or Appraised Value	Allocation	
Land	$ 100,000	100/1350 x $1,215,000 =	90,000
Buildings	600,000	600/1350 x $1,215,000 =	540,000
Equipment	300,000	300/1350 x $1,215,000 =	270,000
Inventory	350,000	350/1350 x $1,215,000 =	315,000
Total	$1,350,000		$1,215,000

NON-MONETARY EXCHANGES

Property, plant, and equipment assets are often acquired by exchanging (for example, trading in) assets other than cash as full or partial payment for the assets being acquired. The general rule is that the acquired asset should be recorded at the fair market value of the asset given up or the asset acquired, whichever is more clearly evident, with any gain or loss on the exchange being recognized. The gain or loss is the difference between the fair market value used and the book value of the asset given up. There are exceptions to this general rule, and they are described below.

An exchange of dissimilar assets (for example, equipment for land) is considered **the completion of the earnings process**. Such exchanges are accounted for by the general rule. To illustrate:

A company trades a piece of equipment for land.

Fair market value of equipment $25,000
Book value of equipment
    Cost $30,000
    Accumulated depreciation   10,000
        Book value $20,000

Following the general rule, the land would be recorded at

$25,000 (market value of asset given up) and a gain of $5,000 would be recognized ($25,000 less book value of $20,000).

The entry to record the exchange would be:

Land	25,000	
Accumulated depreciation, equipment	10,000	
Equipment		30,000
Gain on exchange of assets		5,000

An exchange of similar assets (for example, one item of equipment for a similar item) is considered **not the completion of the earnings process**, and special rules apply. If the exchange results in an apparent **loss** (the fair value of the asset received is less than the book value of the asset given up), the acquired asset is recorded at fair value and the loss recognized. If the exchange results in an apparent **gain** (the fair value of the asset acquired is more than the book value of the asset given up), the acquired asset is recorded at the book value of the asset given up and the gain is **not recognized.**

For example, assume one item of equipment is exchanged for a similar item.

Fair value of equipment acquired	$20,000	
Book value of equipment given up	Cost	$30,000
	Acc. depreciation	8,000
	Book value	$22,000

Since there is an apparent loss on the exchange (the fair value of the equipment received is less than the book value of the equipment given up), the fair value of the equipment acquired would be used and a loss recognized.

Entry:

Equipment	20,000	
Accumulated depreciation, equipment	8,000	
Loss on exchange of assets	2,000	
Equipment		30,000

But, if the fair value of the equipment acquired was $25,000, the book value would be used and no gain recognized.

Entry:

Equipment	22,000	
Accumulated depreciation, equipment	8,000	
Equipment		30,000

If an exchange of similar assets also involves the receipt of cash (boot), any apparent gain is recognized on the cash portion of the transaction. The gain recognized is the amount the cash received exceeds a pro rata portion of the book value of the asset given up.

For example, assume that, in addition to the new equipment with a market value of $25,000 (in the example immediately above), $6,250 cash is received.

Pro rata portion of book value of old equipment:

$$\frac{Cash}{Cash + MV \text{ of asset acquired}}$$

$6,250 / $6,250 + $25,000 = 20%

20% x $22,000 = $4,400

Gain recognized: $6,250 - $4,400 = $1,850

New asset recorded at remaining book value:
$22,000 x 80% = $17,600

Entry:

Cash	6,250	
Equipment	17,600	
Accumulated depreciation, equipment	8,000	
Equipment		30,000
Gain on exchange of assets		1,850

If similar assets are exchanged and cash is paid, the new asset is recorded as the sum of the book value of the old asset plus the cash paid, not to exceed the market value of the new asset. Thus, if the market value is greater than the sum, no gain is recognized. However, if the market value is less than the sum of the book value plus the cash, a loss is recognized.

A **donation** of an asset to an entity is considered a **nonreciprocal transfer.** The acquired asset should be recorded at its fair market value.

Assets acquired by a corporation in exchange for the issuance of equity securities should be recorded at the market value of the securities issued or the asset acquired, whichever is more reliably determinable. If neither has a reliable market value, the value to be recorded for the assets is usually determined by the board of directors.

7.2 DEPRECIATION

Depreciation is the process of allocating the cost of property, plant, and equipment assets to the periods which benefit from the use of the assets. The cost of an asset is allocated over its useful life in a systematic and rational manner.

The variables which are involved in the depreciation process are (1) the historical cost of assets, (2) the estimated residual or scrap value of the assets, (3) the estimated service or useful life, and (4) the depreciation method. Periodic depreciation is recorded by debiting appropriate expense accounts and crediting a contra asset account **Accumulated Depreciation**. The cost of an asset minus its accumulated depreciation is called its **book value**.

Several methods of computing depreciation have been developed. The major methods are:

Straight line
Units of service or production
Sum-of-the-years'-digits
Declining balance

The **straight line method** of depreciation allocates the cost of an asset equally over the periods of the asset's useful life. The useful life is stated in terms of time.

$$\text{Annual Straight line Depreciation} = \frac{\text{Asset Cost} - \text{Estimated Salvage Value}}{\text{Useful Life (in years)}}$$

EXAMPLE: Asset cost = $20,000
        Estimated salvage value = $2,000
        Estimated useful life = 6 years

Annual depreciation = ($20,000 − $2,000)/6 = $3,000

The **units of production method** states the asset's useful

81

life in units of production or service rather than time. The annual depreciation charge then is based on the use of the asset during that year.

$$\text{Depreciation Expense Per Unit of Service} = \frac{\text{Annual Cost} - \text{Estimated Salvage Value}}{\text{Useful Life (in units of service)}}$$

EXAMPLE: Asset (equipment) cost = $20,000
Estimated salvage value = $2,000
Estimated useful life = 6,000 hours of service

Depreciation per unit of service = ($20,000 − $2,000)/6,000 = $3 per hr.

Assume the equipment is used 1,850 hours in 19x1. The depreciation expense for 19x1 = 1,850 x $3 = $5,550.

The **sum-of-the-year's-digits method** and the **declining balance method** are examples of **accelerated depreciation methods.** These methods allocate more of the cost as depreciation in the early years of an asset's life, mainly on the theory that new assets have greater service potential.

The sum-of-the-year's-digits method applies a declining fraction against an asset's cost less salvage value. The denominator of the fraction is the sum of the digits of the asset's useful life. For example, for an asset with a 5-year useful life the sum would be $1 + 2 + 3 + 4 + 5 = 15$. The numerator would be the digits in reverse order. That is, for the first year of the asset's life, the numerator would be 5 and the fraction 5/15.

EXAMPLE: Asset cost = $35,000
　　　　　Estimated salvage value = $5,000
　　　　　Estimated useful life = 5 years
　　　　　Sum-of-the-years'-digits = 1 + 2 + 3 + 4 + 5 = 15

Depreciation under sum-of-the-years'-digits method:

Year	Depreciation Expense	Accum. Dep.	Book Value
1	($35,000 – $5,000) x 5/15 = $10,000	$10,000	$25,000
2	($35,000 – $5,000) x 4/15 =　 8,000	18,000	17,000
3	($35,000 – $5,000) x 3/15 =　 6,000	24,000	11,000
4	($35,000 – $5,000) x 2/15 =　 4,000	28,000	7,000
5	($35,000 – $5,000) x 1/15 =　 2,000	30,000	5,000

The declining balance method applies a fixed percentage against a declining book value. The percentage used is a multiple of the straight line percentage. The rate usually ranges from a high of double the straight line rate (usually called the **double declining balance method**) to 150% of the straight line rate. The selected rate is multiplied each year by the declining book value.

EXAMPLE: Asset cost = $20,000
　　　　　Estimated salvage value = $2,000
　　　　　Estimated useful life = 5 years

　　　　　Straight line depreciation rate = 1/5 = 20%
　　　　　Double declining balance rate = 2 x 20% = 40%

Depreciation under the declining balance method, using a rate double the straight line rate:

Year	Depreciation Expense	Accum. Dep.	Book Value
1	$20,000 x 40% = $8,000	$ 8,000	$12,000
2	$12,000 x 40% = $4,800	$12,800	$ 7,200
3	$ 7,200 x 40% = $2,880	$15,680	$ 4,320
4	$ 4,320 x 40% = $1,728	$17,408	$ 2,592
5	$592*	$18,000	$ 2,000

* Asset cannot be depreciated below its salvage value.

Some companies find it expedient to account for depreciation for groups of assets rather than individual assets. There are several group depreciation systems that may be used.

If a group of assets consists of a large number of items each having a small unit cost, the **inventory system** might be used for depreciation. A record is kept of the cost of assets acquired in the group. At the end of an accounting period, an inventory is taken. The difference between the cost of the inventoried items and the accumulated asset cost is recorded as depreciation expense, with a credit to the asset account.

Under the **retirement system,** the cost of assets is recognized as depreciation expense when they are retired. This method is useful in situations where the assets consist of a large number of identical items which are continually being retired and replaced. A good example is utility poles of an electric utility company. Under the retirement system, no record of individual items is kept, there is no accumulated depreciation account, and no depreciation expense is recognized until units are retired and replaced.

EXAMPLE: Utility Poles account balance Jan. 1 = $325,000
Original cost of poles retired during year = $66,000
Replacement cost of poles retired during year
= $101,000.

Entries:

Depreciation Expense	66,000	
Utility Poles		66,000
Utility Poles	101,000	
Cash		101,000

A similar system is the **replacement system**. Under this system, the debit to depreciation expense is the replacement cost rather than the original cost of the assets replaced. Using the data from the example immediately above, the entry would be:

Depreciation Expense	101,000	
Cash		101,000

The retirement and replacement systems do not properly match the cost of long-lived assets to the periods in which the benefit from their use is obtained. These systems provide a reasonable approximation of an appropriate allocation of cost only when there is a constant retirement and replacement of assets on a continuous basis.

Group and **composite depreciation systems** allocate depreciation for a group of assets on the basis of an average depreciation rate for the group. If the assets in a group are similar, the term used is **group**. If the assets are dissimilar, the term is **composite**. The depreciation rate used is determined as the total annual depreciation for individual assets in the group as a percentage of the total cost of the assets in the group. Upon disposal of an asset in the group, the cost of the asset is debited to the accumulated depreciation. No gain or loss is recognized. The cost of new assets added to the group is debited to the asset account. Occasional revision of the depreciation rate may be needed as the makeup of the group changes.

EXAMPLE

Assume the following asset group.

ASSET GROUP 101:

Component	Cost	Salvage Value	Dep. Cost	Useful Life (Yrs.)	Annual SL Dep.
101.1	$ 50,000	$ 5,000	$45,000	5	$ 9,000
101.2	100,000	10,000	90,000	3	30,000
101.3	70,000	7,000	63,000	7	9,000
Totals	$220,000	$22,000	$198,000		$48,000

Composite depreciation rate = $48,000/$220,000 = 21.8%

Composite useful life = $220,000/$48,000 = 4.58 years

Depreciation entry, Year 1:

Depreciation Expense	48,000	
Accumulated Depreciation,		
Asset Group 101		48,000

At the end of Year 2, an asset in the group that cost $10,000 is sold for $6,000. The retirement entry would be:

Cash	6,000	
Accumulated Depreciation,		
Asset Group 101	4,000	
Asset Group 101		10,000

A consistent policy should be adopted in accounting for depreciation for fractional parts of a year relating to assets acquired or disposed of during the year. Policies commonly used include:

1. Recording depreciation to the nearest whole month — full month's depreciation for acquisitions in first half of month or disposal in second half; no depreciation for acquisitions in second half of month or disposal in first half.

2. Recording a full year's depreciation in year of acquisition and none in year of disposal.

3. Recording a half-year's depreciation in year of acquisition and year of disposal.

7.3 POST-ACQUISITION EXPENDITURES

During the service life of the property, plant, and equipment assets, expenditures are often required to maintain or improve the usefulness of the assets. Those expenditures which are normal in maintaining the usefulness of the asset should be charged to expense. Those expenditures which are expected to increase or extend the usefulness of an asset in future periods should be **capitalized**, that is, recorded as assets and depreciated.

ORDINARY REPAIRS AND MAINTENANCE

Ordinary repair and maintenance expenditures are those needed to maintain the current usefulness of plant and equipment assets. Such expenditures are ordinarily reported as expense in the year in which they are incurred.

If monthly or quarterly financial statements are desired and repair and maintenance expenditures are not evenly distributed during the year, accrual of this expense may be appropriate. An estimate of the total expense for the year is made and allocated monthly or quarterly as expense, with credits to an allowance account. As actual expenditures are made, the allowance account is debited. At the end of the year, any balance in the allowance account is ~~written off~~ *write down* to increase or decrease the expense for the year.

ILLUSTRATION

Assume a company estimates its total repair and maintenance expense for the year will be $24,000, to be incurred at various times during the year. Financial statements are to be prepared monthly.

Monthly accrual entry:

Repair and Maintenance Expense	2,000	
Allowance for Repairs and Maintenance		2,000

Entry when expenditures are actually made:

Allowance for Repairs and Maintenance	xxx	
Cash (or other account)		xxx

Assume a credit balance of $1,820 in allowance account at the end of the year. The adjusting entry:

Allowance for Repairs and Maintenance	1,820	
Repair and Maintenance Expense		1,820

EXTRAORDINARY REPAIRS, REPLACEMENTS, AND BETTERMENTS

Extraordinary, non-recurring expenditures on a plant and equipment asset which extend the useful life or increase the usefulness of the asset should be capitalized.

88

Extraordinary repairs are usually major expenditures beyond normal repairs that extend the useful life of an asset or increase its usefulness. An example would be a major overhaul of an engine in a truck or piece of equipment that extends the useful life of the equipment. The costs of extraordinary repairs that extend an asset's useful life are usually debited to the accumulated depreciation account. If the repair increases the usefulness of the asset, the cost would be debited to the asset account. In either case, the book value of the asset is increased and depreciated over the remaining life of the asset.

EXAMPLE

Assume an asset with the following balances on January 1:

Cost	$40,000
Accum. depreciation	20,000
Book value	$20,000

Remaining useful life on January 1: 4 years
Estimated salvage value: $4,000
Straight line depreciation rate: $4,000 per year

On January 12, extraordinary repairs costing $14,000 are completed. The repairs are expected to increase the useful life of the asset as of January 1, to 6 years.

Accumulated Depreciation, Equipment	14,000	
Cash (or other account)		14,000

Revised book value: $40,000 − $6,000 = $34,000
Revised straight line depreciation rate:
($34,000 − $4,000)/6 = $5,000 per year

A **replacement** or **betterment** involves the removal of a component of an asset and replacement with a component which extends the useful life (replacement) or increases the usefulness (betterment) of the asset. If the book value of the replaced component is known, it should be removed from the accounts, with recognition of gain or loss on disposal. The cost of the new component should then be debited to the asset account. If the book value of the removed component is not known or separately accounted for, the cost of a replacement should be debited to the accumulated depreciation and the cost of a betterment to the asset account.

The costs of **rearrangements** or **relocations** of plant and equipment assets, if material, should be capitalized if the benefits extend beyond the current period and expensed currently if they do not.

7.4 DISPOSAL OF PROPERTY, PLANT, AND EQUIPMENT ASSETS

When a plant and equipment asset is disposed of, a gain or loss on disposal should be recognized on the basis of the difference between the asset's book value and the proceeds of the disposal. Before recording the disposal, depreciation should be recognized for the current year up to the date of the disposal, following the company's policy for fractional year depreciation.

ILLUSTRATION

Assume the following asset balance on January 1:

Cost	$8,000
Accumulated depreciation	2,400
Book value	$5,600
Annual straight line depreciation rate	$1,200

The company recognizes depreciation for fractional years to the nearest whole month.

On March 18, the asset is sold for $6,000.
Entry to record deprecation on the asset for the year:

Depreciation Expense	300	
(3/12 x $1,200)		
Accumulated Depreciation, Equipment		300

Entry for disposal of the asset:

Cash	6,000	
Accumulated Depreciation, Equipment	2,700	
Equipment		8,000
Gain on Disposal of Equipment		700

A plant and equipment asset may be **abandoned**, with no proceeds to the owner. The asset and related accumulated depreciation should be removed from the accounts, with a loss recognized for the book value of the asset.

An **involuntary conversion** occurs when an asset is lost for reasons not the choice of the owner. Examples are losses to casualties such as fire or flood. If there are no proceeds from insurance or salvage, the accounting parallels that for abandonments. If insurance or salvage proceeds are received, the accounting would follow that used for other disposals involving the receipt of cash.

Plant and equipment assets may also be disposed of in a **nonmonetary transaction**. The accounting for such transactions was presented earlier in this chapter.

7.5 NATURAL RESOURCES

Natural resources, such as deposits of oil, coal, ore, and precious metals, may be owned by a company. The acquisition cost for such resources is recorded as an asset.

Depletion is the allocation of the cost of a natural resource deposit against revenue as the resource is extracted and sold. The depletion rate usually is based on the cost of the asset related to the units of production expected from the resource.

EXAMPLE

Assume a deposit of a mineral is acquired at a cost of $3,000,000. The purchaser estimates that 600,000 tons of the mineral can be extracted economically.

Depletion rate: $3,000,000 / 600,000 = $5 per ton

Assume that in year 19x3 150,000 tons are extracted.

Depletion for 19x3 = 150,000 x $5 = $750,000

Entry:

Inventory	750,000	
Mineral deposit		750,000

Alternatively, the credit could be to Accumulated Depreciation, an account contra to the asset.

CHAPTER 8

INTANGIBLE ASSETS

8.1   TYPES OF INTANGIBLE ASSETS

Intangible assets are long-lived assets that lack physical substance but have probable future economic benefit through their use in the production of revenue.

Intangible assets are often classified as **identifiable** or **unidentifiable**. Identifiable intangible assets have separate identities and can be bought or sold separately. Examples are patents and copyrights. Unidentifiable intangible assets cannot be separated from the owning entity and thus cannot be bought or sold separately. The major example is goodwill.

Intangible assets also may be classified as **externally acquired** or **internally developed**.

Externally acquired intangible assets are recorded at their acquisition cost: those costs associated with acquiring the rights to the benefits represented by the asset. For internally developed identifiable intangible assets, only those costs directly related to establishing the **rights** are capitalized. Research and development costs are expensed in conformity with **SFAS 2**. Costs associated with internally developed unidentifiable intangible assets are expensed as incurred.

The cost of an intangible asset acquired on or after **November 1, 1970**, is **amortized**, or allocated, over its useful life, not to exceed 40 years. The cost of an intangible asset acquired before November 1, 1970, is amortized only if the asset has a limited life.

8.2 IDENTIFIABLE INTANGIBLE ASSETS

PATENTS

A **patent** is a right granted by government which gives the holder the exclusive right to make, use, or sell the item covered by the patent. The legal life of a patent is 17 years.

The cost of an externally acquired patent should be capitalized as an asset. Costs associated with the registration application for an internally developed patent should be capitalized. The research and development costs associated with the item covered by the patent are expensed as incurred in accordance with **SFAS 2**. The cost of a successful legal defense of a patent should be capitalized.

A patent is an asset only as long as the right granted has future economic benefit. The cost of a patent should be amortized over the patent's economic life or its legal life, whichever is shorter.

COPYRIGHTS

A **copyright** grants exclusive rights to a literary or artistic work. The legal life of a copyright is the life of the author plus 50 years. Accounting for copyrights is similar to that for patents. The cost of a copyright should be amortized over the copyright's economic life or 40 years, whichever is shorter.

94

TRADEMARKS

Trademarks are distinguishing symbols, phrases, or other devices used for product or company identification. Registration of a trademark provides exclusive use indefinitely, since the registration is renewable. The cost of a trademark should be amortized over its economic life or 40 years, whichever is shorter.

FRANCHISES

A **franchise** is an agreement in which one party (the **franchisor**) grants a second party (the **franchisee**) the right to sell certain products or services or perform other functions. For example, a city government may grant a franchise for the furnishing of electricity within the city, or a company such as McDonald's may grant a franchise for a restaurant in a particular location.

The initial cost of obtaining a franchise should be recorded as an asset and amortized over the life of the franchise or 40 years, whichever is shorter.

8.3 UNIDENTIFIABLE INTANGIBLE ASSET: GOODWILL

Goodwill is the ability of an enterprise to earn an above-normal return on its operations. This ability is usually related to such qualities as good reputation, good location, highly skilled work force, and exceptional managerial ability.

Goodwill is an unidentifiable intangible asset. It is recorded as an asset only when it is externally acquired in a business combination accounted for as a purchase. When one company purchases another, goodwill is recognized to the extent that the total purchase price exceeds the fair market value of the identifiable net assets acquired.

The cost of recognized goodwill should be amortized over its expected economic or useful life, not to exceed 40 years.

The negotiations over a purchase price for the acquisition of another company may involve estimating the value of goodwill. Theoretically, the current value of goodwill for a given entity is the present discounted value of the expected future excess earnings.

EXAMPLE

Assume negotiations for the purchase of a company. A study of recent years' earnings and projected trends indicate the company can expect a return of 20% on the current value of its assets of $300,000. Research indicates that the normal return expected for companies of this type in this industry is 14%.

Estimated future annual earnings ($300,000 x 20%) $60,000
Estimated normal annual earnings ($300,000 x 14%)   42,000
Estimated excess annual earnings $18,000

Assume that this excess earning ability will continue for 5 years.

Goodwill   = Present value of $18,000 discounted 14% (cost of capital) for 5 years

         = 3.43308 ($18,000) = $61,795

8.4   OTHER INTANGIBLE ASSETS

DEFERRED CHARGES

A **deferred charge** is a long-term prepaid expense. Examples are long-term prepaid insurance and plant rearrangement costs. A deferred charge should be amortized over its life, which is likely to be much less than the maximum of 40 years.

ORGANIZATION COSTS

Costs incurred in the formation of a corporation, such as legal fees and stock underwriting costs, are often recorded as an intangible asset called **organization costs**. These costs are typically amortized over the first few years of the corporation's existence.

RESEARCH AND DEVELOPMENT COSTS

Research and development costs are those costs incurred for activities such as basic research, new product development, and product or process improvement. Although such activities may result in future economic benefit, identifying a direct relationship between a particular expenditure and future benefit is usually difficult. The FASB therefore requires in **SFAS 2** that research and development costs be expenses in the period incurred.

DEVELOPMENT STAGE ENTERPRISES

The **development stage** for an enterprise is the period in which activities are centered around establishing the new business. Planned principal operations have not commenced or have not begun to produce significant revenue. An issue is whether some costs that normally would be expensed should be capitalized as intangible assets during the development stage of an enterprise. **SFAS 7** requires that development stage enterprises present their financial statements on the same basis as other entities. Costs should be capitalized only if they would otherwise qualify as assets. The standard does require that the financial statements be identified as those of a development stage enterprise and that any accumulated deficit be identified on the balance sheet as "Deficit accumulated during development stage." Additional special disclosures are required for these companies.

97

OIL AND GAS EXPLORATION COSTS

Oil and gas companies usually incur significant costs in exploring for oil and gas deposits. Many wells are usually drilled in order to locate an oil or gas reserve. Many of the wells will be "dry holes" that strike no oil or gas deposit. A major accounting issue is whether the cost of drilling unsuccessful wells should be capitalized or not.

Two methods of accounting for oil and gas exploration costs are used. The **successful-efforts method** capitalizes only the cost of successful wells. The costs associated with "dry holes" are expensed as incurred. In the **full-cost method** all exploration costs are capitalized and amortized against the revenue from the successful wells.

The FASB issued **SFAS 19,** which would have required the use of the successful-efforts method as the only acceptable method. However, for various reasons, the FASB subsequently suspended this pronouncement. Therefore, both the successful-efforts and full-cost methods are currently acceptable for financial reporting.

COSTS OF COMPUTER SOFTWARE TO BE MARKETED

Accounting issues have arisen concerning the costs of developing and marketing computer software. The major issue is whether the costs of developing computer software for sale or lease should be expensed or capitalized. The FASB, in **SFAS 86,** requires that costs incurred prior to the establishment of **technological feasibility** for the product be expensed as research and development costs. Technological feasibility is established upon completion of the product design or a working model of the product. Costs incurred from the date of technological feasibility until the date of general release of the software product should be capitalized and amortized over the expected life of the product. Production costs for the product after general release should be accounted for as inventory.

"The ESSENTIALS" of
ACCOUNTING & BUSINESS

Each book in the **Accounting and Business** ESSENTIALS series offers all essential information about the subject it covers. It includes every important principle and concept, and is designed to help students in preparing for exams and doing homework. The **Accounting and Business** ESSENTIALS are excellent supplements to any class text or course of study.

The **Accounting and Business** ESSENTIALS are complete and concise, with quick access to needed information. They also provide a handy reference source at all times. The **Accounting and Business** ESSENTIALS are prepared with REA's customary concern for high professional quality and student needs.

Available titles include:

Accounting I & II	**Financial Management**
Advanced Accounting I & II	**Income Taxation**
Advertising	**Intermediate Accounting I & II**
Auditing	**Microeconomics**
Business Law I & II	**Macroeconomics I & II**
Business Statistics I & II	**Marketing Principles**
Corporate Taxation	**Money & Banking I & II**
Cost & Managerial Accounting I & II	

If you would like more information about any of these books,
complete the coupon below and return it to us or go to your local bookstore.

REA's Test Preps
The Best in Test Preparation

- REA "Test Preps" are far **more** comprehensive than any other test preparation series
- Each book contains up to **eight** full-length practice exams based on the most recent exams
- **Every** type of question likely to be given on the exams is included
- Answers are accompanied by **full** and **detailed** explanations

REA has published over 60 Test Preparation volumes in several series. They include:

Advanced Placement Exams (APs)
Biology
Calculus AB & Calculus BC
Chemistry
Computer Science
English Language & Composition
English Literature & Composition
European History
Government & Politics
Physics
Psychology
Spanish Language
United States History

College Level Examination Program (CLEP)
American History I
Analysis & Interpretation of Literature
College Algebra
Freshman College Composition
General Examinations
Human Growth and Development
Introductory Sociology
Principles of Marketing

SAT II: Subject Tests
American History
Biology
Chemistry
French
German
Literature

SAT II: Subject Tests (continued)
Mathematics Level IC, IIC
Physics
Spanish
Writing

Graduate Record Exams (GREs)
Biology
Chemistry
Computer Science
Economics
Engineering
General
History
Literature in English
Mathematics
Physics
Political Science
Psychology
Sociology

ACT - American College Testing Assessment

ASVAB - Armed Service Vocational Aptitude Battery

CBEST - California Basic Educational Skills Test

CDL - Commercial Driver's License Exam

CLAST - College Level Academic Skills Test

ELM - Entry Level Mathematics

ExCET - Exam for Certification of Educators in Texas

FE (EIT) - Fundamentals of Engineering Exam

FE Review - Fundamentals of Engineering Review

GED - High School Equivalency Diploma Exam (US & Canadian editions)

GMAT - Graduate Management Admission Test

LSAT - Law School Admission Test

MAT - Miller Analogies Test

MCAT - Medical College Admission Test

MSAT - Multiple Subjects Assessment for Teachers

NTE - National Teachers Exam

PPST - Pre-Professional Skills Tests

PSAT - Preliminary Scholastic Assessment Test

SAT I - Reasoning Test

SAT I - Quick Study & Review

TASP - Texas Academic Skills Program

TOEFL - Test of English as a Foreign Language

RESEARCH & EDUCATION ASSOCIATION
61 Ethel Road W. • Piscataway, New Jersey 08854
Phone: (908) 819-8880

Please send me more information about your Test Prep Books

Name _____

Address _____

City _____ State _____ Zip _____

"The ESSENTIALS" of Math & Science

Each book in the ESSENTIALS series offers all essential information of the field it covers. It summarizes what every textbook in the particular field must include, and is designed to help students in preparing for exams and doing homework. The ESSENTIALS are excellent supplements to any class text.

The ESSENTIALS are complete and concise with quick access to needed information. They serve as a handy reference source at all times. The ESSENTIALS are prepared with REA's customary concern for high professional quality and student needs.

Available in the following titles:

Advanced Calculus I & II
Algebra & Trigonometry I & II
Anatomy & Physiology
Anthropology
Astronomy
Automatic Control Systems /
   Robotics I & II
Biology I & II
Boolean Algebra
Calculus I, II & III
Chemistry
Complex Variables I & II
Data Structures I & II
Differential Equations I & II
Electric Circuits I & II
Electromagnetics I & II

Electronics I & II
Electronic
   Communications I & II
Finite & Discrete Math
Fluid Mechanics /
   Dynamics I & II
Fourier Analysis
Geometry I & II
Group Theory I & II
Heat Transfer I & II
LaPlace Transforms
Linear Algebra
Math for Engineers I & II
Mechanics I, II & III
Microbiology
Modern Algebra

Numerical Analysis I & II
Organic Chemistry I & II
Physical Chemistry I & II
Physics I & II
Pre-Calculus
Probability
Psychology I & II
Real Variables
Set Theory
Statistics I & II
Strength of Materials &
   Mechanics of Solids I & II
Thermodynamics I & II
Topology
Transport Phenomena I & II
Vector Analysis

If you would like more information about any of these books,
complete the coupon below and return it to us or go to your local bookstore.

HANDBOOK of
**MATHEMATICAL,
SCIENTIFIC, &
ENGINEERING**
FORMULAS, FUNCTIONS,
GRAPHS, TABLES,
& TRANSFORMS

RE A RESEARCH & EDUCATION ASSOCIATION

A particularly useful reference for those in math, science, engineering and other technical fields. Includes the most-often used formulas, tables, transforms, functions, and graphs which are needed as tools in solving problems. The entire field of special functions is also covered. A large amount of scientific data which is often of interest to scientists and engineers has been included.

Available at your local bookstore or order directly from us by sending in coupon below.

"The ESSENTIALS" of COMPUTER SCIENCE

REA's **Problem Solvers**

The "PROBLEM SOLVERS" are comprehensive supplemental text-books designed to save time in finding solutions to problems. Each "PROBLEM SOLVER" is the first of its kind ever produced in its field. It is the product of a massive effort to illustrate almost any imaginable problem in exceptional depth, detail, and clarity. Each problem is worked out in detail with a step-by-step solution, and the problems are arranged in order of complexity from elementary to advanced. Each book is fully indexed for locating problems rapidly.

ACCOUNTING
ADVANCED CALCULUS
ALGEBRA & TRIGONOMETRY
AUTOMATIC CONTROL
    SYSTEMS/ROBOTICS
BIOLOGY
BUSINESS, ACCOUNTING, & FINANCE
CALCULUS
CHEMISTRY
COMPLEX VARIABLES
COMPUTER SCIENCE
DIFFERENTIAL EQUATIONS
ECONOMICS
ELECTRICAL MACHINES
ELECTRIC CIRCUITS
ELECTROMAGNETICS
ELECTRONIC COMMUNICATIONS
ELECTRONICS
FINITE & DISCRETE MATH
FLUID MECHANICS/DYNAMICS
GENETICS
GEOMETRY

HEAT TRANSFER
LINEAR ALGEBRA
MACHINE DESIGN
MATHEMATICS for ENGINEERS
MECHANICS
NUMERICAL ANALYSIS
OPERATIONS RESEARCH
OPTICS
ORGANIC CHEMISTRY
PHYSICAL CHEMISTRY
PHYSICS
PRE-CALCULUS
PROBABILITY
PSYCHOLOGY
STATISTICS
STRENGTH OF MATERIALS &
    MECHANICS OF SOLIDS
TECHNICAL DESIGN GRAPHICS
THERMODYNAMICS
TOPOLOGY
TRANSPORT PHENOMENA
VECTOR ANALYSIS

If you would like more information about any of these books,
complete the coupon below and return it to us or visit your local bookstore.

RESEARCH & EDUCATION ASSOCIATION
61 Ethel Road W. • Piscataway, New Jersey 08854
Phone: (908) 819-8880

Please send me more information about your Problem Solver Books

Name _____

Address _____

City _____ State _____ Zip _____